Thomas Bock

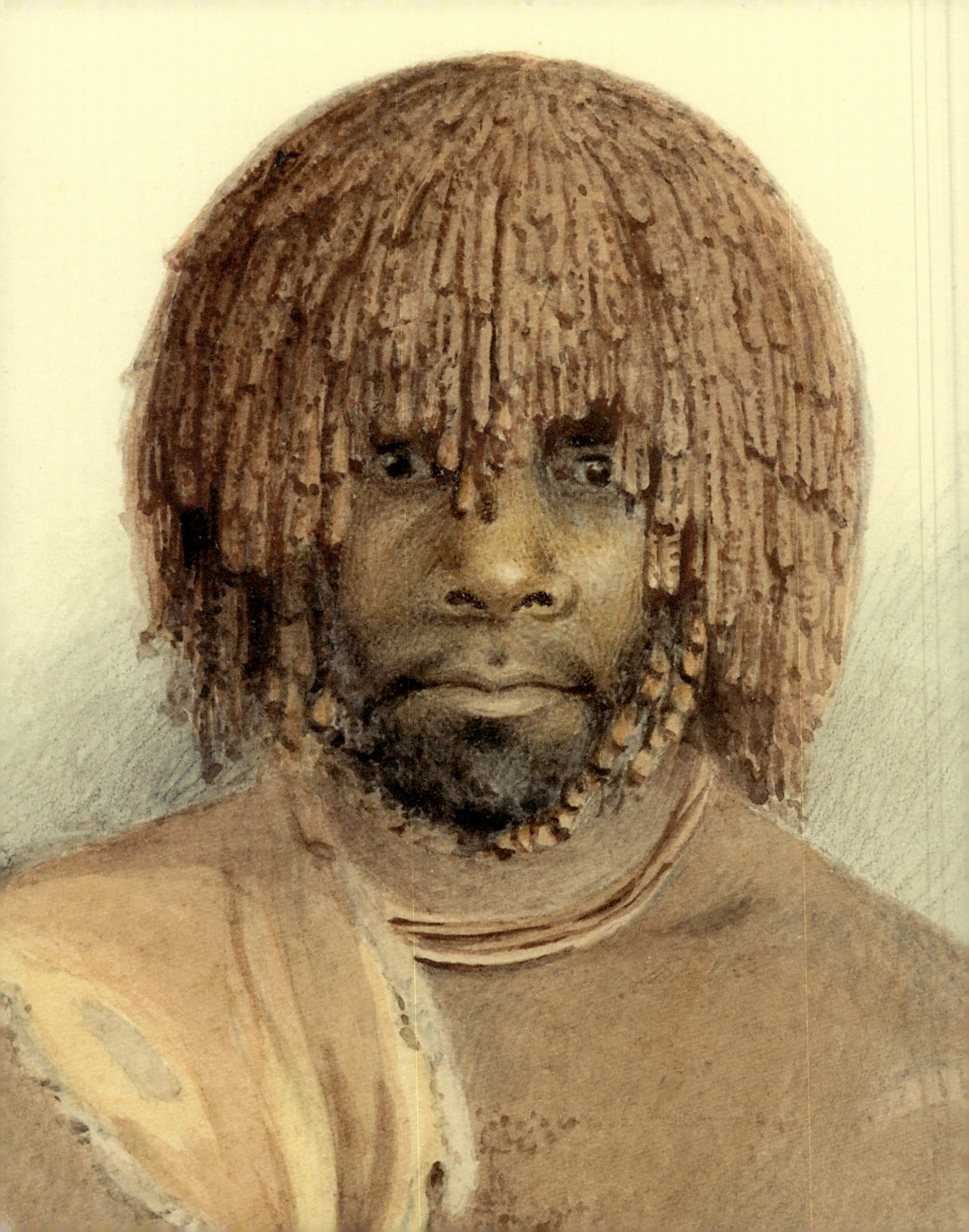

Thomas Bock

IKON

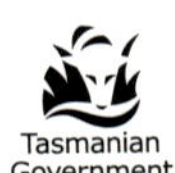

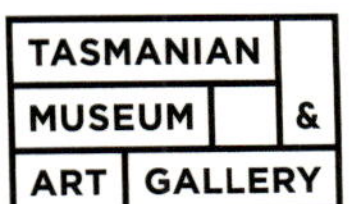

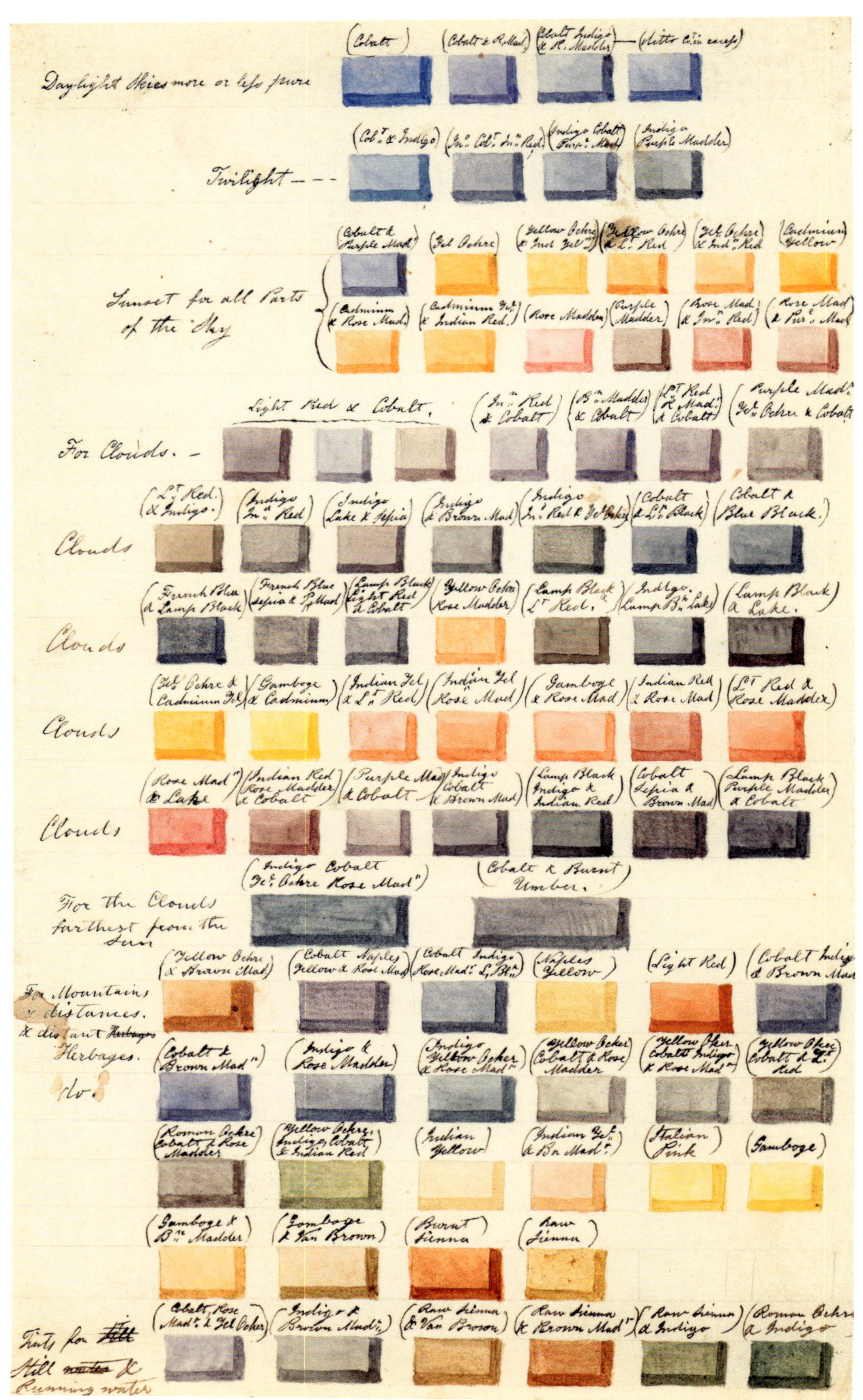

Personal colour chart, undated

Contents

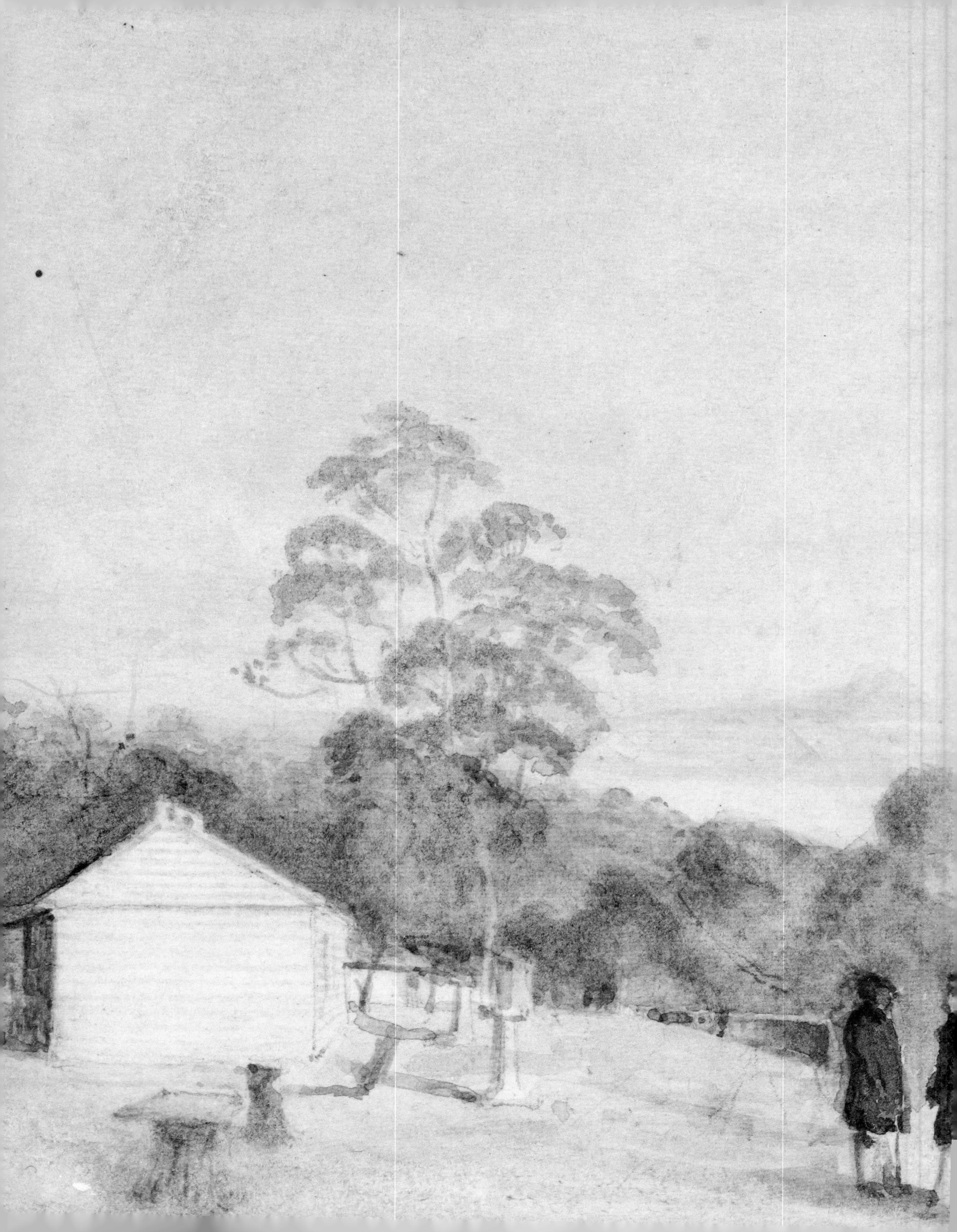

Foreword

This is the first exhibition dedicated to the work of Thomas Bock (c. 1793–1855) since 1991, and the first ever outside of Australia. It comprises a selection of drawings, paintings and photographs that demonstrate not only the artist's technical skill, but also his sensitivity to a wide range of subject matter including portraits of Tasmanian Aborigines, his fellow criminals as well as free settlers in Hobart Town, nudes, landscapes and everyday scenes, occasionally giving touching insight into his domestic life.

Bock was one of the most important artists working in Australia during the colonial years. Born in Birmingham, trained there as an engraver and miniature painter, in 1823 he was found guilty of "administering concoctions of certain herbs ... with the intent to cause miscarriage" and sentenced to transportation for fourteen years. He arrived in Hobart the following year where quickly he was pressed into service as a convict artist, engraving banknotes, illustrations for a local almanac and commercial stationery. An early commission was a number of portraits of captured bushrangers, before and after execution by hanging, including the notorious cannibal Alexander Pearce.

In a short space of time, Bock's life was turned upside down. Once a respectable artisan in his early twenties, with a good address in a booming industrial town, he now found himself at the edge of the known world in the company of compatriots who were as desperate as they were depraved. There are no surviving diaries that document his personal journey, but Bock's artistic output, on arrival, through conditional and absolute pardons until his death – marked by an obituary that described him as "an artist of a very high order" – is a rich seam of observation, at once subtle and astonishing.

Most significant in this respect is Bock's series of portraits of Tasmanian Aborigines, commissioned by George Augustus Robinson during 1831–35, now in the British Museum. It is a master set, from which a number of copies were made. The drawing throughout is very fine and the likenesses probably very true, and having them at the heart of this exhibition will effectively convey the tragedies suffered by Indigenous people through the British colonisation of Australia. The sitters – including Trukanini (c. 1812–76) have a demeanour that conveys both pride and despair. For British audiences on the whole this work will be a revelation; for Aboriginal visitors to the exhibition in Hobart – who know the sad narrative only too well – it will be a rare and poignant opportunity to see first-hand such early pictures of their ancestors.

In the longer term, Bock made a living for himself through his portraits of British colonists, usually government officials, wealthy farmers, businessmen and their families. He advertised himself as a "portrait painter", but there are many more drawings that we have chosen for this exhibition as they tend to have a liveliness that is absent from the paintings. Together with the sketches he made in his studio or at home, often of his family, and sometimes outdoors, they are like pieces in a jigsaw of social history. Another fascinating side to Bock's artistic practice is revealed in his life drawing, a number of nude studies that are as tender as they are well observed. Nothing is known of the circumstances in which they were made, and there seems to be nothing else like them in colonial Australian art.

The advent of photography, and in particular the process published by Louis Daguerre in 1839, was a threat to the livelihood of portrait painters. Our exhibition includes some daguerreotypes by Bock depicting the kinds of people that he might previously have drawn or painted, providing further evidence of his openness to new experience, and incorporating it into his existing practice. It is interesting to speculate on what might have happened to Bock had he remained in Birmingham. In Tasmania certainly he became more than a big fish in a small pond, and the body of work by him that survives is remarkable not only for its inherent quality but also the light it shines on the early years of a penal colony in Australia, the aspiration and the awfulness of it. The unintended consequence of probably his only known criminal offence, it amounts to a compelling story that should be more widely known.

Also widely known should be those who provided support without which this exhibition could not have happened. Many thanks to the Australian Government's Department of Foreign Affairs and Trade and to those at the Australian High Commission, especially Alessandra Pretto and HE the Hon Alexander Downer Australian High Commissioner to the United Kingdom. Likewise the Gordon Darling Foundation, Jonathan Ruffer Curatorial Research Grant from Art Fund, Owen Family Trust, The John Feeney Charitable Trust and an anonymous donor have made an enormous difference to what was possible for us; and how much too we appreciate the guidance and advice given by Theresa Sainty, and Heather Sculthorpe and others at the Tasmanian Aboriginal Corporation, the TMAG Aboriginal Advisory Council, and our colleagues at the Allport Library and Museum of Fine Arts, the British Museum, the Queen Victoria Museum and Art Gallery, and the State Library of New South Wales. Above all, we take this opportunity to express our gratitude to esteemed colleagues Hamish Maxwell-Stewart, Professor of Social History at the University of Tasmania; Gaye Sculthorpe, Curator and Section Head of Oceania at the British Museum and Jane Stewart, Principal Curator at the Tasmanian Museum and Art Gallery; not only for their essays herein, but also for their good will and unstinting generosity.

Janet Carding
Director, Tasmanian Museum and Art Gallery

Jonathan Watkins
Director, Ikon

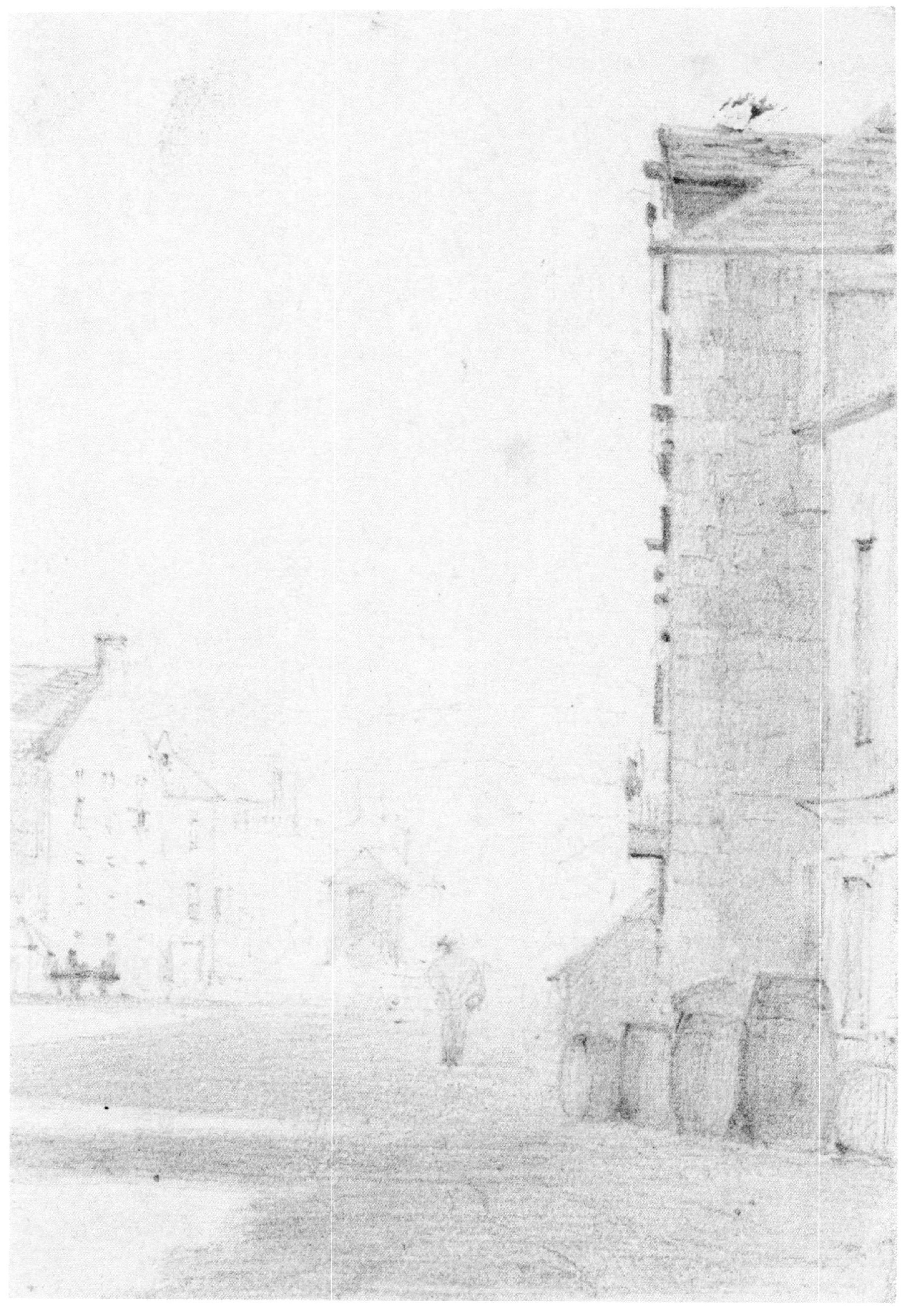

Commissariat Store or Hunter's Wharf, 1830–55

Thomas Bock's Hobart Town

Jane Stewart

Little survives that tells us about Thomas Bock's life in Birmingham.[1] We know he was an aspiring and talented engraver, that he married into a family of printers, and that he had five children with his first wife Charity Broome. He was a chorister at Lichfield Cathedral and from the age of fourteen he was apprenticed to the trade engraver Thomas Brandard.[2] By 1814 he had established his own engraving business and throughout the next decade he worked from addresses in Upper Temple Street, Duddeston Street, Great Charles Street and finally Tower Street. He showed promise and in 1817 was awarded a silver medal from the Society of Arts for an engraving of a portrait. It is also likely that he took art tuition in Birmingham, a theory supported by drawings and quotes in surviving sketchbooks.[3]

Bock's legacy as an artist is based entirely on the work he produced in Tasmania. Comprising mainly of portraits, the surviving collection of images is characterised by careful observation and a deft hand. He emerged successfully from his convict sentence to become one of the most sought after artists in the colony and by the 1830s reviewers were praising him as "talented", "eminent" and an artist of "genius and ability".[4] The eyes of those he portrayed were nearly always bright, emphasising personality and warmth of character, and he is widely thought to be one of the most sensitive and subtle of the colonial artists. With this in mind, it is difficult to reconcile the artist with the crime for which he was transported, and which uprooted him from an established life in Birmingham and delivered him to Hobart.

Bock was arrested in April 1823. He and his accomplice Mary Day Underhill were accused of persuading a seventeen year old girl, Ann Yates, to leave her family home in defiance of her parents. Bock arranged for her lodgings in a private house from where he "affected her seduction", visiting regularly over two years. When Yates became pregnant, Bock and Underhill were charged with "administering decoctions of certain herbs [...] with intent to cause her miscarriage".[5]

When passing the sentence of fourteen years, Justice Park claimed he had "never tried a more wicked and malignant case", and "alluded to the arts [Bock] had practised in seducing the poor girl from the house of her parents to gratify his wicked inclinations, and forcibly remarked on the enormity of his offence, standing in the relation he did as the father of four children, some of whom were daughters."[6] Park also noted the depravity of Bock's attempts to defame Yates by referring to her as a "common street walker" and concluded that had Bock and Underhill "been capitally convicted, he should have considered it his duty not to recommend them as objects of clemency, and must have left them to their fate".[7] Bock was transported on the *Asia* with 149 other convicts. They embarked in Woolwich on 15 July 1823 and arrived in Hobart on 19 January 1824.

While Bock created a remarkable body of commissioned engravings and portraits over the thirty years he was in Hobart, he also left behind a tantalising collection of drawings. Sketchy and often spontaneous, they build a skeletal picture of the world he occupied, as well as likenesses of former convicts and others who experienced varying levels of hardship and prejudice. Two sketchbooks begin in England and follow his journey to Hobart. The drawings in them are frenetically paced and difficult to decipher in the most part but they also provide distinct clues to Bock's life. These images are invaluable documents, unique in Tasmania and more broadly in Australia.

In the early pages of one sketchbook, there is a group of domestic drawings, so small and finely delineated that they are easy to overlook. They include a woman washing clothes, her back turned to two children, and a sketch of four children standing in a line, two playing the violin while a seated woman faces the other way. It is not unreasonable to wonder whether they depict Bock's English family. There is also a view of a city, probably Birmingham.

Poignantly, the same book follows his journey by sea beginning with depictions of

English port towns and coastline, and the dramatic profile of the Cape Verde Islands. There are sketches of waves and the open ocean, a solitary ship, and detailed drawings of Cape Town where rows of orderly buildings are dwarfed by the looming Table Mountain. The sea in these scenes is dead calm, matching the surgeon's account of the "light airs" that "detained [them] off the Cape" for nine days.[8] Later in the sequence is a drawing that could be the coastline of southern Tasmania as it would have been seen by Bock for the first time.

The passage of the sketchbook between England and Australia suggests that it was precious to Bock; that he enjoyed drawing and aspired to move beyond the world of trade engraving and to become an artist. Nevertheless, on arrival in Hobart he was immediately put to work engraving notes for the newly established Bank of Van Diemen's Land. He probably brought tools and materials with him for access to specialist equipment was limited in the colonies.[9] It is uncertain who he was assigned to first – it might have been the Naval

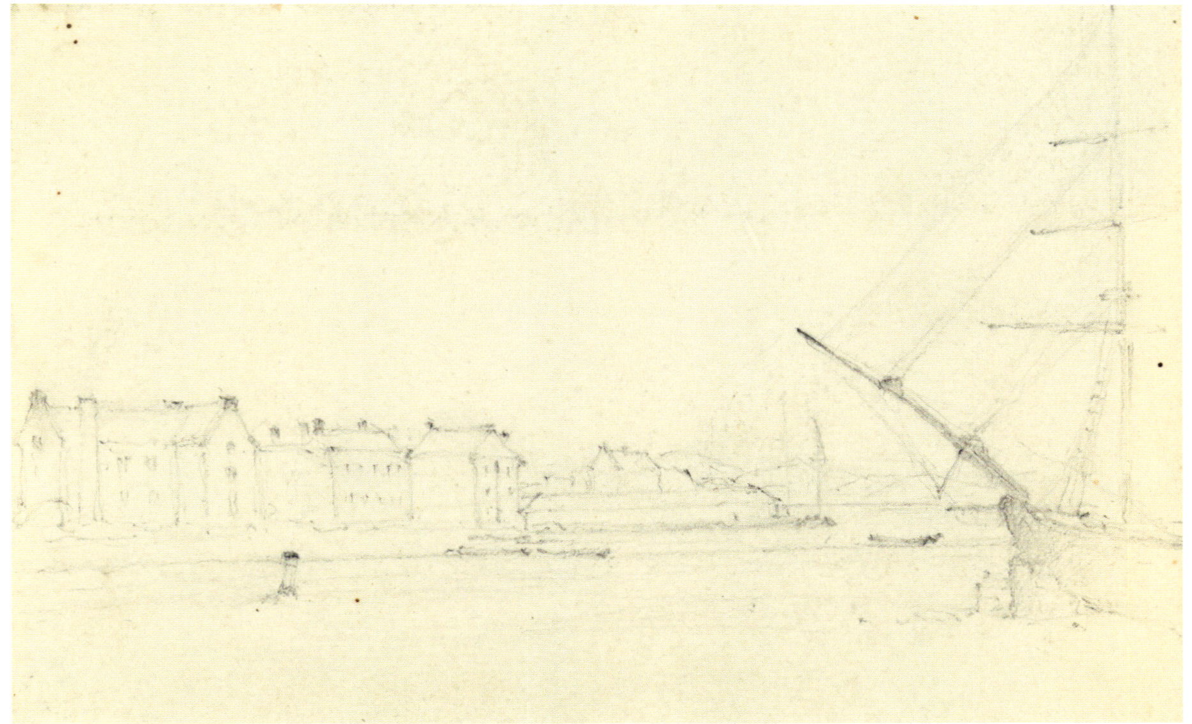

Sketch of Old Wharf, Hobart Town view from the commissariat store, 1830–55

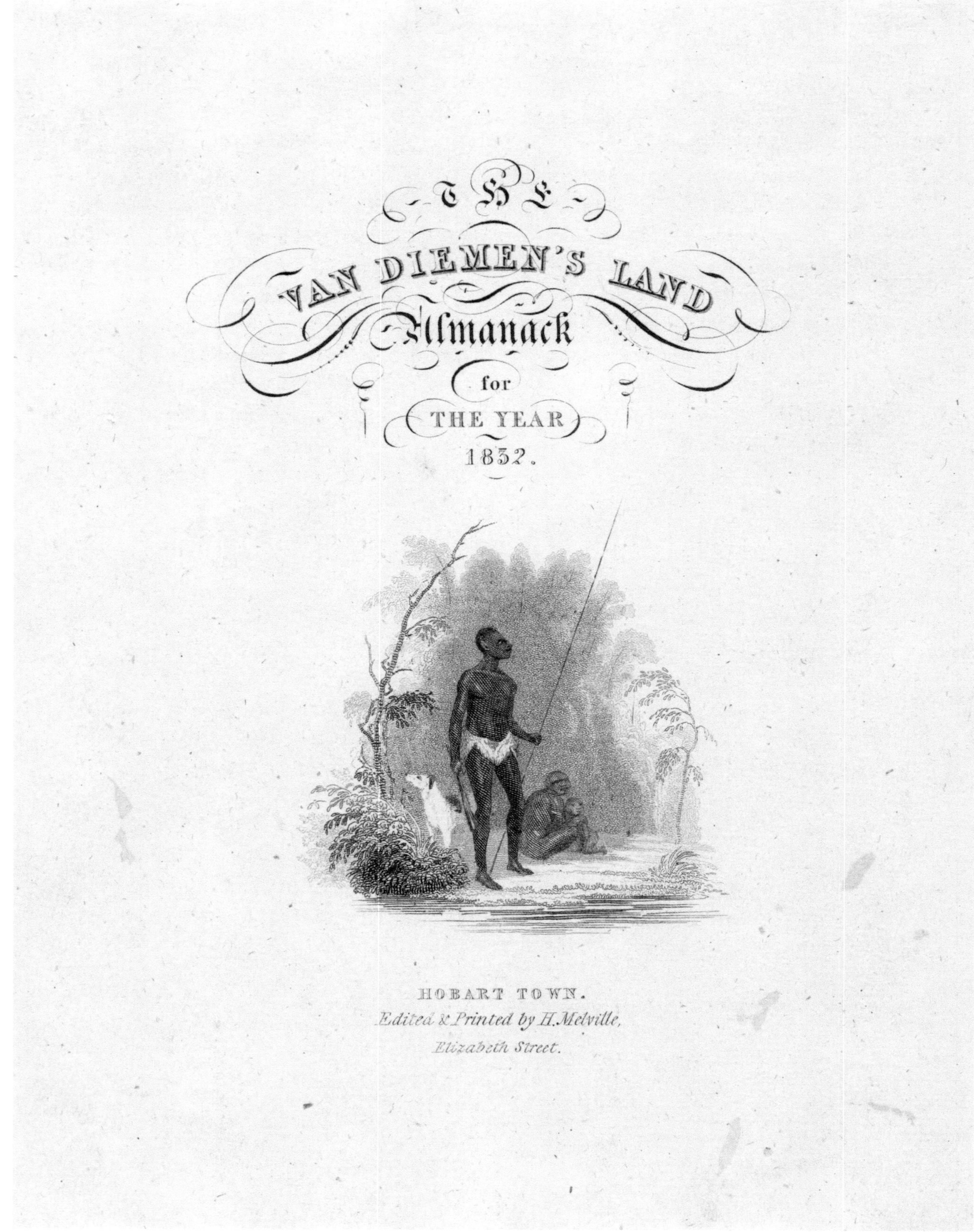

Cover of Van Diemen's Land Almanac for the year 1832, 1832

Officer Edward Bromley who was dismissed for embezzlement in 1824. As early as 1825, Bock advertised in Andrew Bent's *Tasmanian Almanack* as a "Portrait Painter, Historical and Writing Engraver" working in Bathurst Street. In the same year, he was briefly assigned to the Deputy Surveyor George Evans who was an artist and art teacher, and son-in-law of Thomas Lempriere, also an amateur artist and a government official who was well connected in the colony. We can only speculate on what these connections may have meant to Bock.[10]

Bock's skills were highly regarded and he played a vital role in the development of the colonial economy by designing and engraving bank notes for three different banks, producing bill heads, trade and invitation cards, and engraving the illustrations for the local almanacs.[11] He regularly produced work for the government printers and also for the colonial surgeon James Scott. Bock received his Absolute Pardon after more than eleven years in Hobart, in August 1835.

Seven months after Bock's arrival in Hobart, Scott asked him to draw Alexander Pearce (c. 1790–1824) who was condemned to death following the murder and cannibalism of fellow convict escapee Thomas Cox. Pearce's crimes were widely known and studies of his head were deemed valuable in physiognomic circles. However, despite Scott's "scientific" intent and the sensationalism surrounding Pearce, Bock's post-mortem portrayals are surprisingly passive depictions that do not appear to exaggerate features or bend to public perception. They are entirely without caricature and if it were not for the bruise under the neck, Pearce might be mistaken for any sleeping man.

The drawings of Pearce were the first in a series of convicted criminals. Over the next two decades, Bock attended many court trials where he produced images of seventeen Tasmanian bushrangers in all. They were sketched in a thronging courtroom where the men were not formally sitting for him, which might account for their slight clumsiness in comparison to other portraits by Bock. Nevertheless, in this candid state the bushrangers seem harmless enough: young, clean shaven and well dressed in collared shirts. There is nothing extreme about them and if their crime and situation were unknown they might be mistaken for a free and easygoing group of lads. The exceptions are the four images drawn after execution, and the three-part engraving of Charles Routley: his face in life and death, and his skull after dissection.

The images of Pearce and the *Sketches of Tasmanian Bushrangers* remained with Bock throughout his life and it is not fully understood why he pursued these likenesses so persistently. Although Scott's request for Pearce's image may have prompted the series, and the images of the other executed men were also the result of an official request, the remaining pictures seem to have been initiated by Bock himself. Bock's stepson Alfred claimed that Bock was working on a book about the bushrangers at the time of his death, and Andrew Sayers referenced a collection of "original documents, police reports and depositions" about the bushrangers that was acquired with the folio.[12] Whatever propelled this fascination, these portraits capture a group of men at their most desperate and it must be considered that the convict in Bock felt some compassion towards them. Ironically, at least from a contemporary perspective, the petty theft for which Pearce and nearly all of the bushrangers were originally transported seems mild in comparison to Bock's abuse of Ann Yates.

In comparison to the harsh sentences dealt to bushrangers and other criminals (there were no less than 103 executions in Hobart in 1826–27),[13] Tasmanian Aborigines faced persecution on a devastating and genocidal scale. Between 1831 and 1835 Bock painted fourteen Tasmanian Aboriginal people, commissioned by the Government-appointed Conciliator, George Augustus Robinson for a book that was never published. Bock's portrayals are among the most sensitive images of Aboriginal people produced at the time and, as Gaye Sculthorpe writes in her essay elsewhere in this publication, they are "significant cultural documents" for Aboriginal people today.[14]

Over the next decade, Bock reproduced at least five series based on the original portraits; however it is the initial images that reveal the most about each person. This series also includes the only surviving likenesses of Multiyalakina (Eumarrah), Tukalunginta (Togerlongerter) and a man thought to be Muntipiliyata (Montpelliater). All three men were leaders and among the last Aboriginal people to be captured after years of outwitting colonists.[15] There is an immediacy about the three images that indicates they were sketched in real life. Watercolour and some detail is in their faces but not their bodies and, unlike the others pictured by Bock, they are not wearing kangaroo skins. They were not used to the close presence of Europeans and unsurprisingly, Multiyalakina's shoulders are raised in an awkward way, suggesting he is uncomfortable under Bock's scrutiny.[16] These are raw and intense portraits that also imply Bock may have produced equally candid sketches before working up the other portraits into the finished images. Nonetheless, Bock's portraits of Aboriginal people sit well apart from the cruder, less detailed, and far less expressive images of Tasmanian Aboriginal people by other colonial artists working in Hobart.[17] While it cannot be forgotten

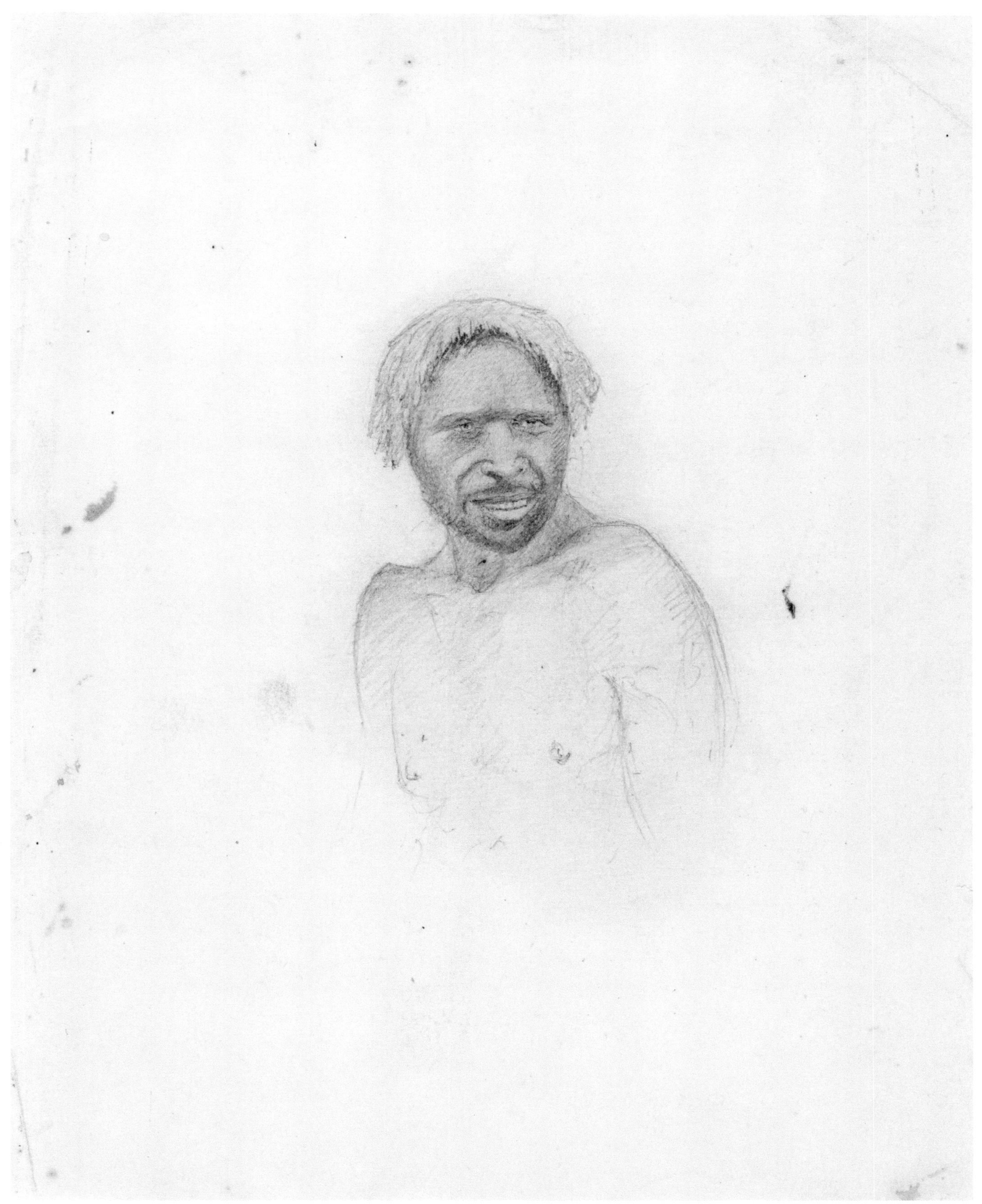

Untitled, probably **Tukalunginta** (Togerlongeter), early 1830s

that Bock was paid to produce these images, and that he would have been aware of their potential to further his reputation, they are also the most truthful and considered of the colonial portraits of the first Tasmanians.[18]

In 1842 the Lieutenant-Governor's wife, Jane Franklin, asked Bock to portray Mithina (Mathinna), the orphaned Aboriginal child she had "adopted" three years before. The portrait is perhaps his best known image, its power testament to both Mithina's vivacity, which was documented by visitors to Government House, and the dexterity of the artist.[19] Nearly two centuries later, the strength of the portrait is considered the main reason Mithina features prominently in Tasmanian history.[20]

Jane Franklin mentions the image in a letter to her sister, describing Mithina as a child who "in spite of every endeavour, and although entirely apart from [her] own people, retains much of the unconquerable nature of the savage; extreme uncertainty of will and temper, great want of perseverance and attention, little if any self-control, and great acuteness of the senses and facility of imitation."[21] In contrast however, Bock depicts Mithina as a calm child who seems perfectly comfortable within his presence. It is a felt image and her intense gaze suggests she is engaged with Bock and the portrait process. Her hands are held loosely together and her head is upright. The fashionable red dress represents her place in a privileged household, although the bare feet, which were concealed by an oval mount for more than a century, reflect her resistance to shoes and possibly British convention. The level of detail suggests that Bock took great care with this portrait, probably because of the Franklin's influence but also, just maybe, because he was responding to Mithina as a person. Interestingly, like the bushranger images, he held onto her portrait until his death and Jane Franklin sent a different copy to her family in England.[22]

Around this time, Bock met Mary Ann Cameron (née Spencer), also a former convict who was about 24 years younger than him. By 1843 they were living together with Henry and Alfred, Mary Ann's children from a former marriage.[23] They were married in 1850 and five children were born between 1843 and 1853: Edwin, William, Frederick, Walter and Arthur. Edwin died in 1853.

A group of small pencil sketches, compelling for their intimacy, create a trace record of their life together. There are several scenes of a woman, presumably Mary Ann, who is sewing and reading with a child crawling under the table, in another she is holding a child, and in several she is sitting as if for a portrait. There are many studies of a woman's hands, children's

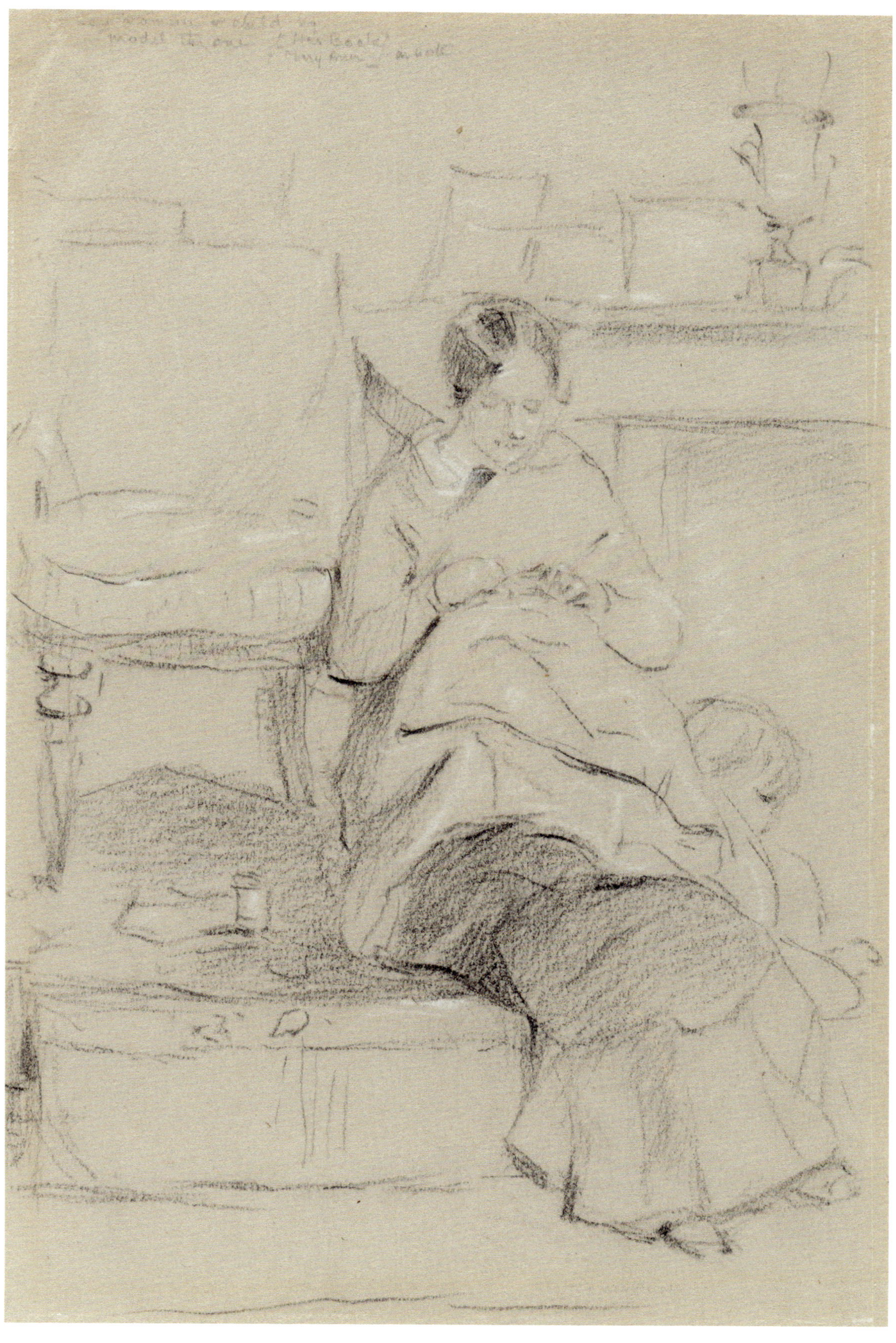

Interior view with woman sewing and child at right, c. 1840

faces, and a child resting his head on a table. In one background there is an armchair on a small dais which is probably where clients sat for their portrait.

Connected to these in style and subject are an extraordinary group of life drawings. The model is similar in appearance to the woman in the domestic scenes and, noting also the level of intimacy in the images, she is thought to be Mary Ann. They are exquisite, fleshly drawings created in Bock's private realm, far removed from the commissions he is better known for. The woman is at ease in his company, her body relaxed and unaffected, and in the reclining poses her eyes level with the viewer. They are the only life drawings to survive from colonial Tasmania and are remarkable for their tenderness and sensuality. Collectively, these images describe a warmth between Thomas and Mary Ann, suggesting a bond that inspired him to draw her throughout their years together in a small house overrun with children, domestic demands and no doubt the pinch of a modest income.

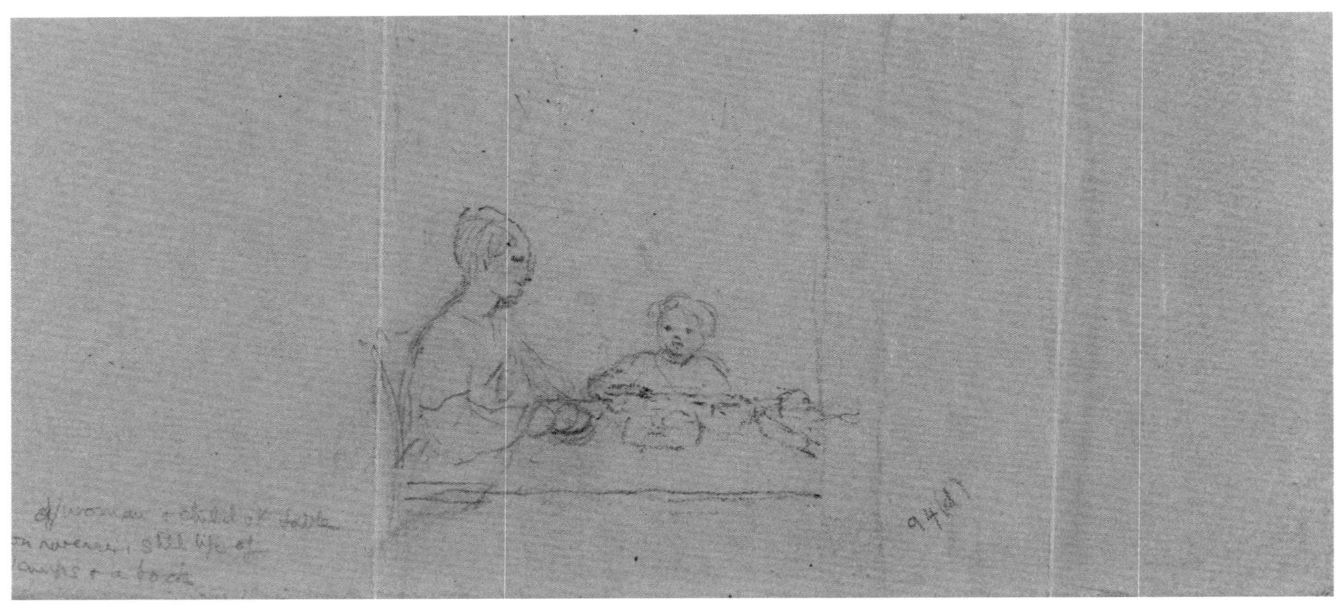

Woman and child at table, c. 1840

Their home must have been open to visitors for it was also the site of Bock's business. One columnist, acidly describing a day in the life of the "indefatigable" Colonial Surveyor George Frankland, wrote that rather than attending to his office he "is to be consulted at the house of that eminent artist Mr. Bock, in Campbell-street, at any hour between ten and three o'clock daily, where he is busily engaged having a full length likeness taken of his exquisite person."[24] While Frankland's portrait is now missing, there is little doubt that Bock would have flattered the Colonial Surveyor, as he did nearly all his clientele.

On the other hand, one of the frankest portraits Bock painted is a watercolour of fellow convict and artist William Buelow Gould. Almost miniature in scale, it stands apart from other likenesses for sheer candidness. Gould's eyes are duller than those in other portraits by Bock and he wears a vacant expression that is emphasised by woolly eyebrows and underlying shadows. An unruly quiff creates an unkemptness, the nose extends to a prominent hook, and the edges of the mouth are set down. This is the closest Bock came to caricature. Gould, an infamous drunk and impoverished reoffender, would not have had the means to commission Bock, and it is most probable that this characterful likeness was the product of a friendship. One can only speculate about the circumstances under which it was drawn, but it was probably completed around 1839 when Gould was living down the road at 4 Campbell Street.

There is scant evidence to show how artists met and interacted in early Hobart; however the town was small and alliances were inevitable. Several artists lived near Bock: Benjamin Duterrau was a direct neighbour, Robin Hood's framing business and gallery was around the corner, as was George Peck's Repository of Fine Arts. Fellow convict and artist Thomas Griffiths Wainewright lived nearby in the Campbell Street Prisoner's Barracks, and later at number 6.

The enigmatic Wainewright was transported to Hobart in 1837, convicted for forgery but infamously suspected of poisoning three family members. In London, he had mixed with the literary and artistic elite, publishing elaborate critiques and exhibiting at the Royal Academy. He also possessed a formidable knowledge of art that he might well have shared with Bock. In Hobart, both Wainewright and Bock were sought after portraitists who excelled in pencil and watercolour and were masters in the gentle manipulation of their subject's image to emphasise elegance and grace. Wainewright undoubtedly influenced the "swan" necks and upturned collars that appeared in Bock's work in the 1840s. While there is little to connect the two further, a draft of Wainewright's 1845 petition for clemency to the Lieutenant-Governor, John Eardley-Wilmot was in Bock's belongings after his death.[25] This suggests that Bock was the calligrapher of Wainewright's lengthy and heartfelt plea, and it paints a compelling scenario of one convict portraitist and aesthete helping another.

Bock's transition from convict to respected artist was no easy feat, almost certainly requiring a great deal of discipline and hard work. In Bock's time Hobart became a cultural place, hosting the first art exhibition in Australia in 1837, followed by others in 1845 and 1846.[26] Bock definitely exhibited in the latter two, and it was probably no coincidence that patronage accelerated for him at this time. Yet his many celebrated portraits of well-to-do colonists are balanced by a singular record of people who were less privileged than his regular clientele. As a collection these are distinctive for not only do they reflect aspects of the life of a convict and artist, but also they are records of an underclass that, with the exception of the Tasmanian Aboriginal people, was rarely pictured. While most of these images have survived in folios, sketchbooks, as small drawings, or even as scraps of paper, the depictions of captured bushrangers, Tasmanian Aborigines, his former-convict friends and wife, their children, and even the post-mortem portraits also discussed in this publication by Hamish Maxwell-Stewart, establish a unique picture of colonial Hobart that is seldom documented. These images were never meant to be displayed as works of art, and they exist in contrast to the hundreds of commissioned, framed portraits Bock created for exhibition and recognition. Arguably they are his greatest legacy.

1
Bock's parents are listed as John Bock and Mary Walpole on Ancestry.com. *England, Select Births and Christenings, 1538–1975* [database on-line]. Provo, UT, USA: Ancestry.com Operation, Inc., 2014. Original data: *England, Select Births and Christenings, 1538 – 1975.* See also Roger Butler, 'Thomas Bock, Engraver', Diane Dunbar (ed.), *Thomas Bock. Society Portraitist, Convict Engraver*, exhibition catalogue, Victoria Museum and Art Gallery Australian National Gallery, Launceston and Canberra: 1991, p.5, for possibilities of Bock's parentage and birth date. The convict record states that Bock was born in Hammersmith, near Lichfield, in 1793 ("by calculation"), but on his death in 1855 he was said to be 65, making his birth date 1790.

2
There are several references to Bock's childhood role as a chorister and his lifelong interest in music. See *Australian Dictionary of Biography*, Volume 1, Melbourne University Press, Melbourne, 1966 and also 'Notes' (thought to be written by Geoffrey Stillwell) in the Thomas Bock file in the Tasmanian Archives and Heritage Office (TAHO) Archives.

3
Two of Bock's sketchbooks from the 1820s suggest that he received art tuition in Birmingham. That in the Tasmanian Museum and Art Gallery collection includes drawings of a femlleum and Art Gallery collection includes studies from *Malton's Perspective* and handwritten quotes from *The Discourses of Sir Joshua Reynolds*.

4
Colonial Times, 20 September 1836, and 30 June 1846; *The Courier*, 9 January 1845.

5
'House of Lords', *Berrow's Worcester Journal*, 10 April 1823.

6
Ibid.

7
Ibid.

8
William Evans, *Medical and surgical journal from the Asia convict ship from 28 June 1823 to 18 January 1824 by William Evans, surgeon and superintendent during which time the said ship was conveying 150 male convicts from Woolwich to Hobart Town, Van Diemen's Land, New South Wales,* National Archives, Kew, United Kingdom, REF ADM 101/4/7 (ancestry.com.uk).

9
Roger Butler, op. cit. p.7.

10
Bock's portrait of William Buelow Gould was presented to the Tasmanian Museum and Art Gallery by Mr H Westbrook, thought to be Thomas Lempriere's grandson, suggesting they were connected in some way.

11
See *Hobart Town Gazette*, 10 December 1824 and *The Sydney Gazette and New South Wales Advertiser*, 13 February 1830, in which Bock's "adept" engraving skills are praised.

Bock produced copperplate engravings for James Ross's *Hobart Town Almanack* in 1829, 1830 and 1835, and Henry Melville's *Van Diemen's Land Almanack* between 1832 and 1834.

12
Andrew Sayers, 'Thomas Bock, Draughtsman', Diane Dunbar (ed.), op.cit. p.25.

13
Ibid, p.26, quoted from Richard Davis, *The Tasmanian Gallows; A Study of Capital Punishment*, Cat and Fiddle Press, Hobart 1974.

14
See N.J.B. Plomley, 'Thomas Bock's portraits of the Tasmanian Aborigines', Diane Dunbar (ed.), op. cit., pp.33–41 for detailed research about these portraits.

15
The *palawa kani* names used here differ from those used by Plomley, Robinson and Bock.

16
Email correspondence with Gaye Sculthorpe, October 2017.

17
Benjamin Duterrau, John Glover, Thomas Napier, Robert Neill, John Skinner Prout, and William Buelow Gould were among the artists who produced images of Tasmanian Aboriginal People.

18
See N.J.B. Plomley, 'Prelude', *Friendly Mission: the Tasmanian Journals and Papers of George Augustus Robinson 1827–1834*, N.J.B. Plomley (ed.), exhibition catalogue, Quintus and Queen Victoria Museum and Art Gallery, Hobart and Launceston 2008, notes 16 and 35, for consideration of portraits by French artist Nicolas-Martin Petit, visiting Tasmania in 1802 with explorer Nicolas Baudin, being of equal significance.

19
See N.J.B. Plomley's references to the letter written by Mithina (Mathinna) and also John Philip Gell's letter to his father, 4 November 1831, in 'Notes on the Tasmanian Aborigines and on portraits of them', *Papers and proceedings of the Royal Society of Tasmania,* Volume 102 – Part II, 1968, pp.50–51.

20
See Penny Russell, 'Girl in a Red Dress: Inventions of Mathinna', *Australian Historical Studies*, Volume 43, Issue 3, 2012, pp.341–362.

21
Letter from Jane Franklin to her sister Mrs Simpkinson, 8 March 1843, quoted in Eve Buscombe, *Artists in early Australia and their portraits,* Eureka Research, Sydney 1978, p.301.

22
Mithina (Mathinna) was presented to the Tasmanian Museum and Art Gallery by Bock's granddaughter, Mrs J. H. Clark, in 1951. The present whereabouts of the Franklin's copy is unknown, although in 1991 Plomley notes that it is in a private collection in England.

23
Bock's response to the *Van Diemen's Land Census of the Year 1843* is in the State Library of Tasmania collection. It tells us that he was renting a brick house at 22 Campbell Street, living with three other 'free' people and nil servants.

24
The Colonial Times, 20 September 1836.

25
Wainewright and Bock exhibited with a group of artists in 1846. See *Catalogue of Paintings, Engravings and Watercolour Drawings, Exhibited at R.V.Hood's New Exhibition Room, Liverpool Street, Hobart Town, in the year MDCCCXLVI* in the Royal Society of Tasmania collection, University of Tasmania.

See Andrew Sayers, op. cit., notes 17 and 30. The finished petition submitted to Eardey-Wilmot is in the Mitchell Library, State Library of New South Wales, Sydney.

26
See Joan Kerr, 'The status of art in Van Diemen's Land', *The Bulletin of the Centre for Tasmanian Historical Studies,* Vol. 1, No. 3, 1987, pp.17–33.

See *Catalogue of Paintings, Watercolour Drawings and Engravings exhibited in the Legislative Council Chambers, Hobart Town, in the year MDCCCXLV* in the State Library of Victoria Collection, and *Catalogue of Paintings, Engravings and Watercolour Drawings, Exhibited at R.V.Hood's New Exhibition Room,* op. cit.

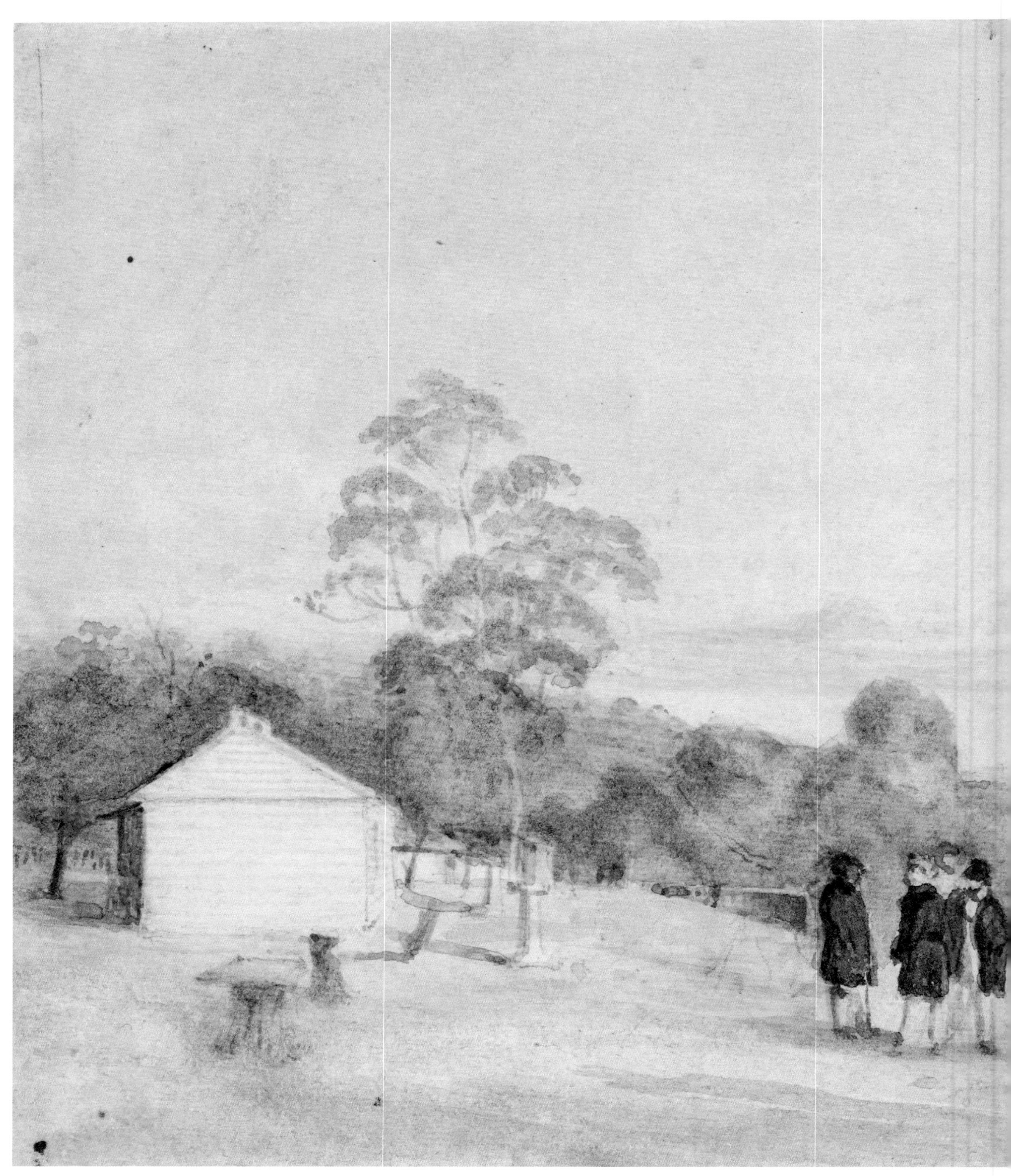

Observatory, Domain, Sir John Franklin, Captain Crozier and Captain James Ross, RN, 1842

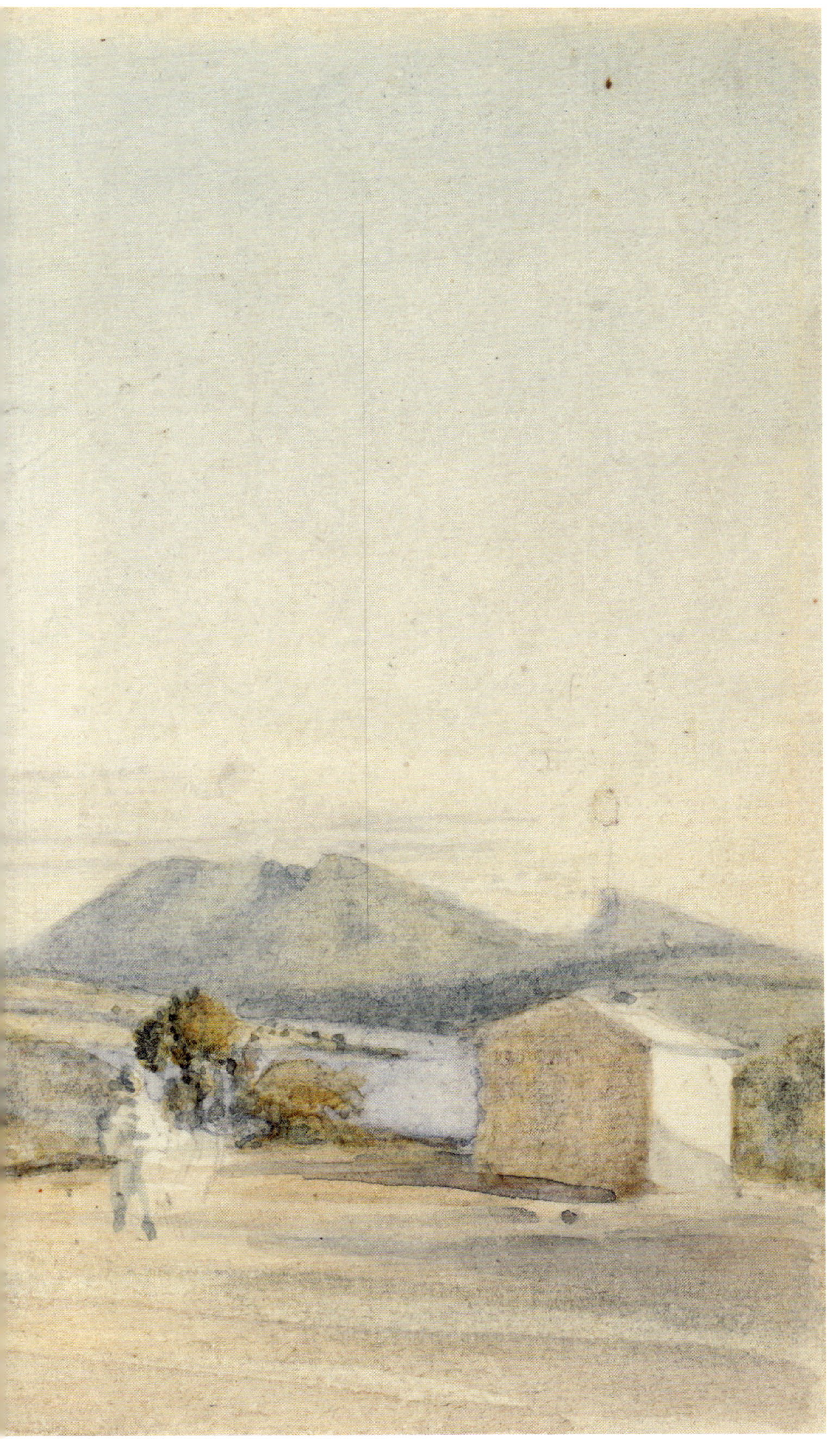

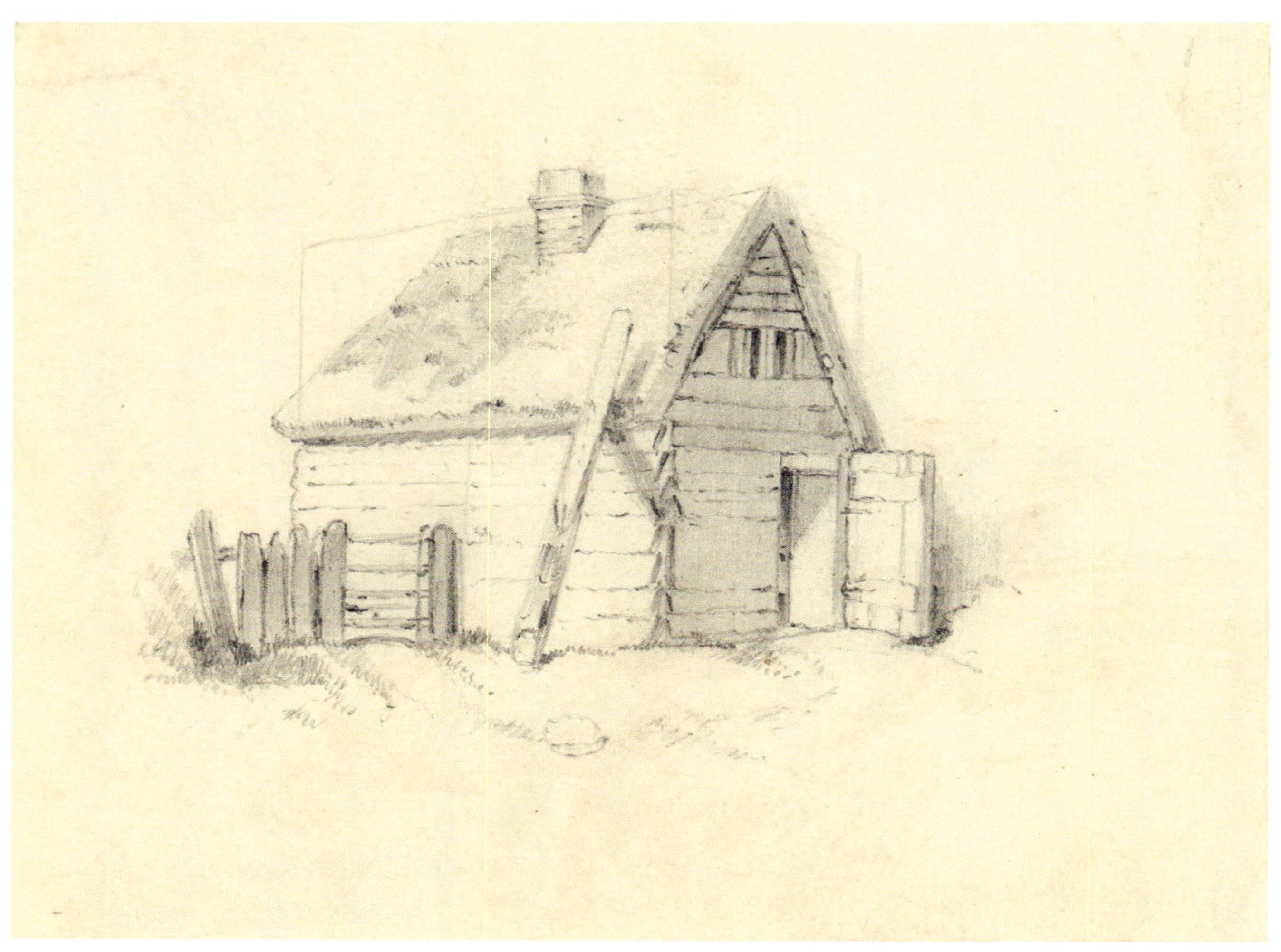

Sketch of a shed, 1824–55

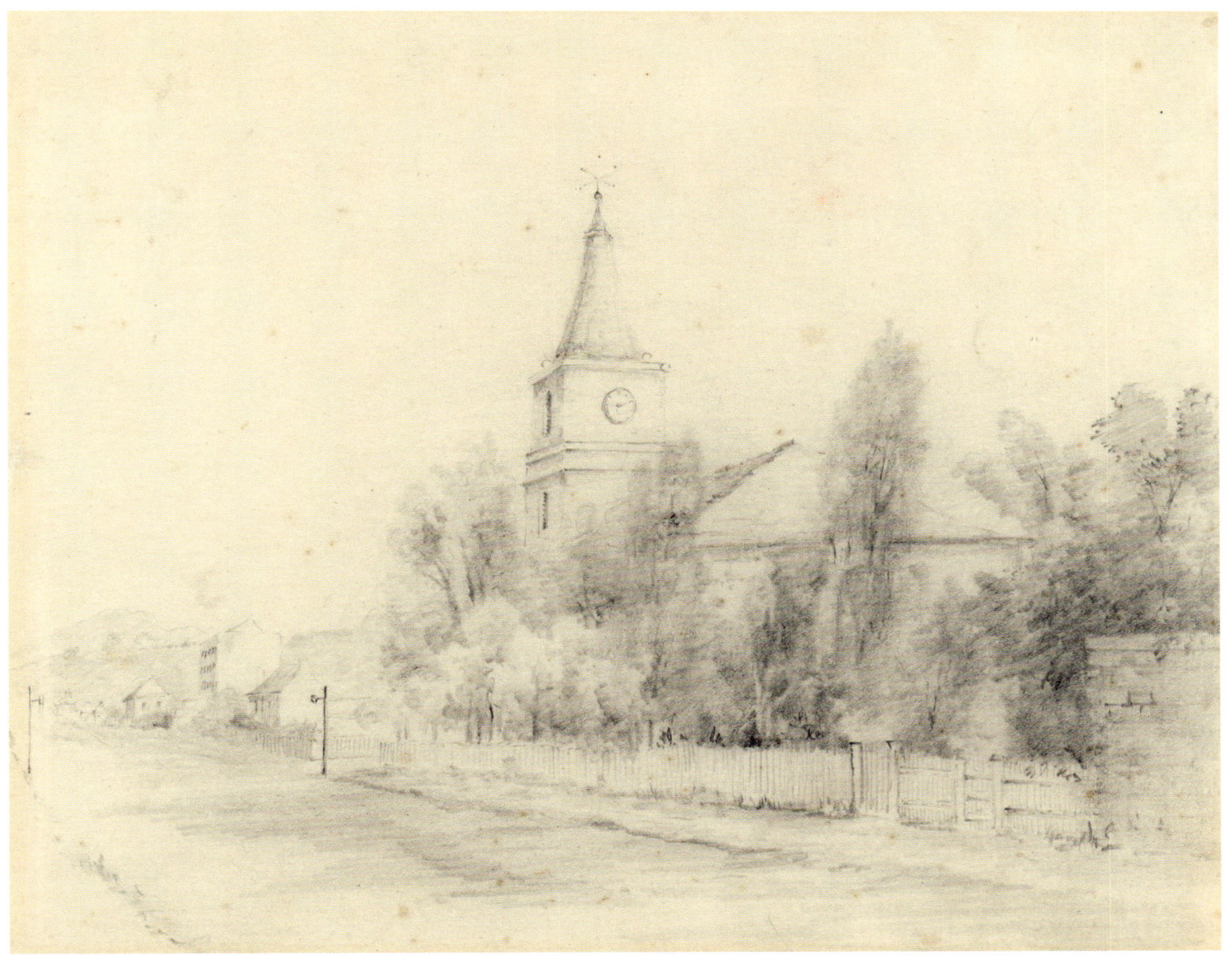

St David's Church, Hobart Town, 1824–35

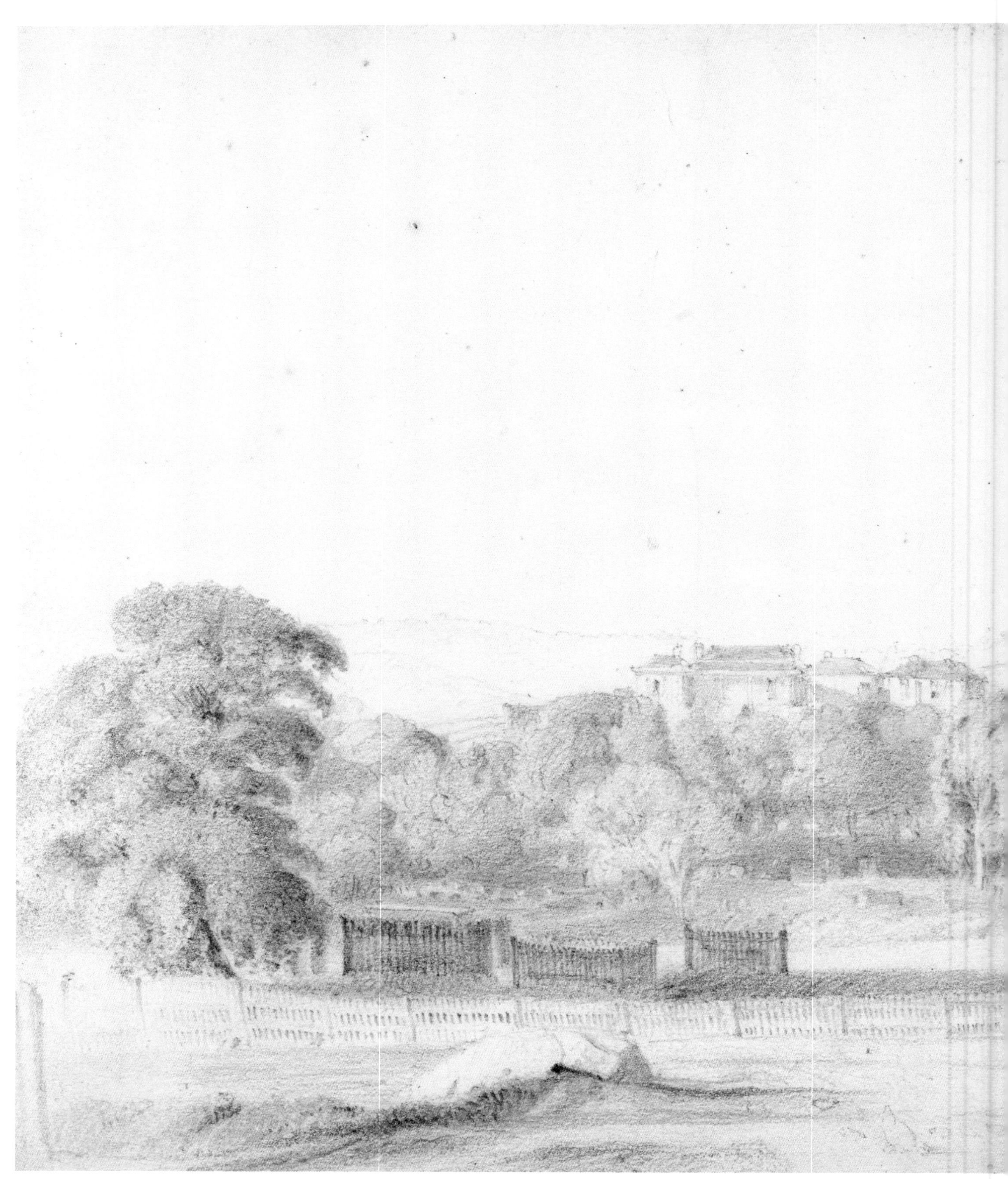

Page from **Sketchbook of post mortem studies**, c. 1835

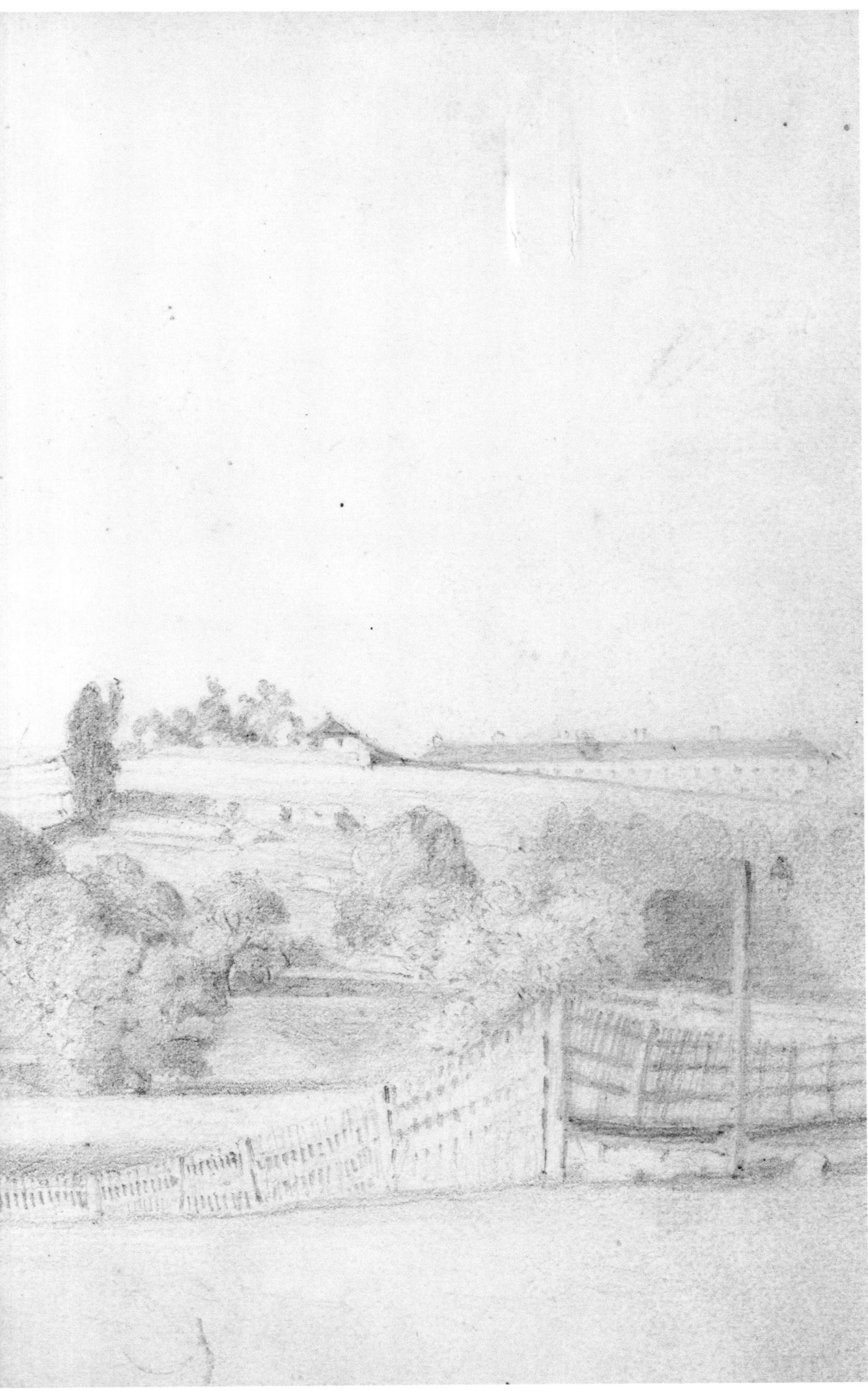

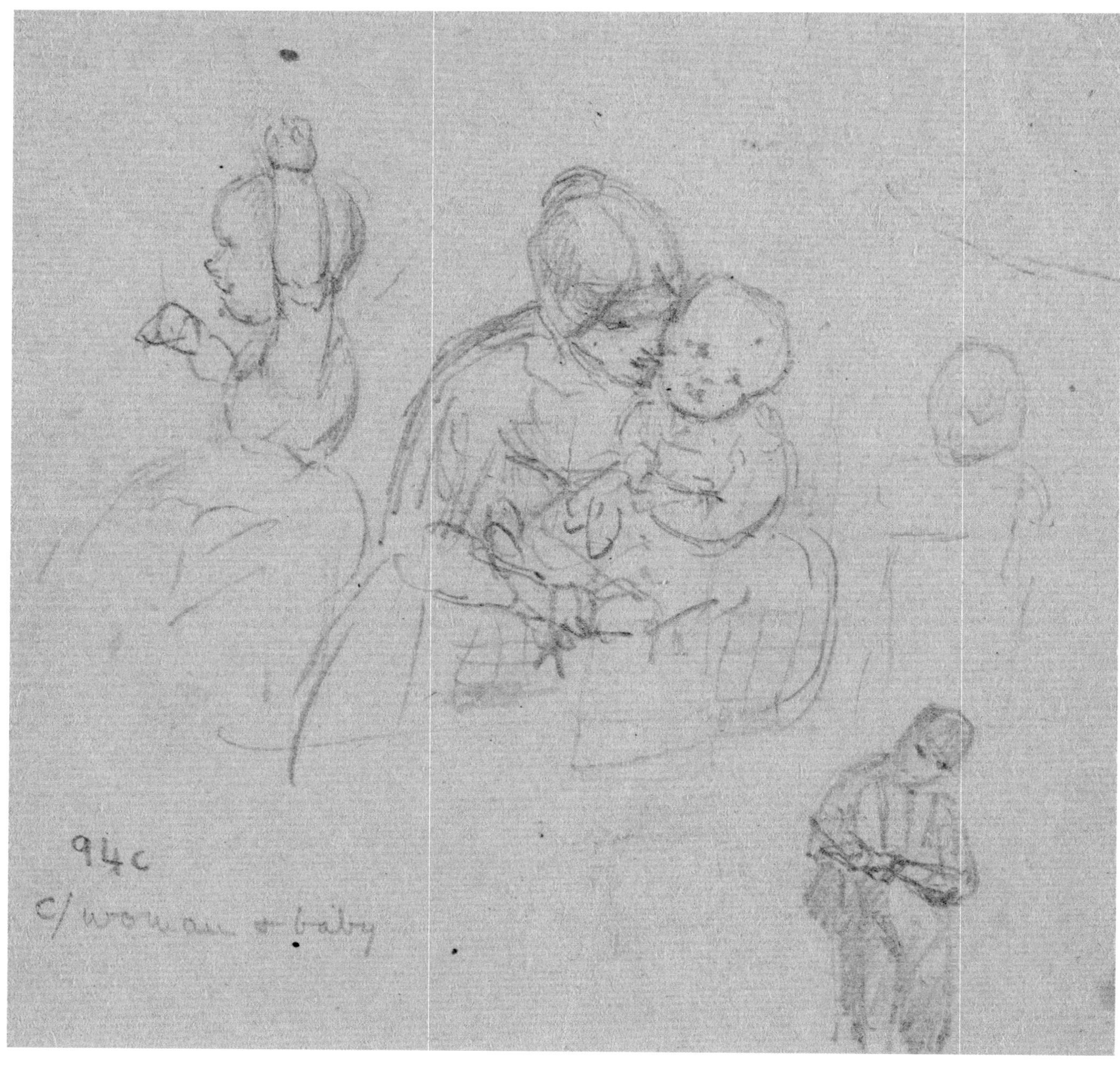

Woman and baby, c. 1840

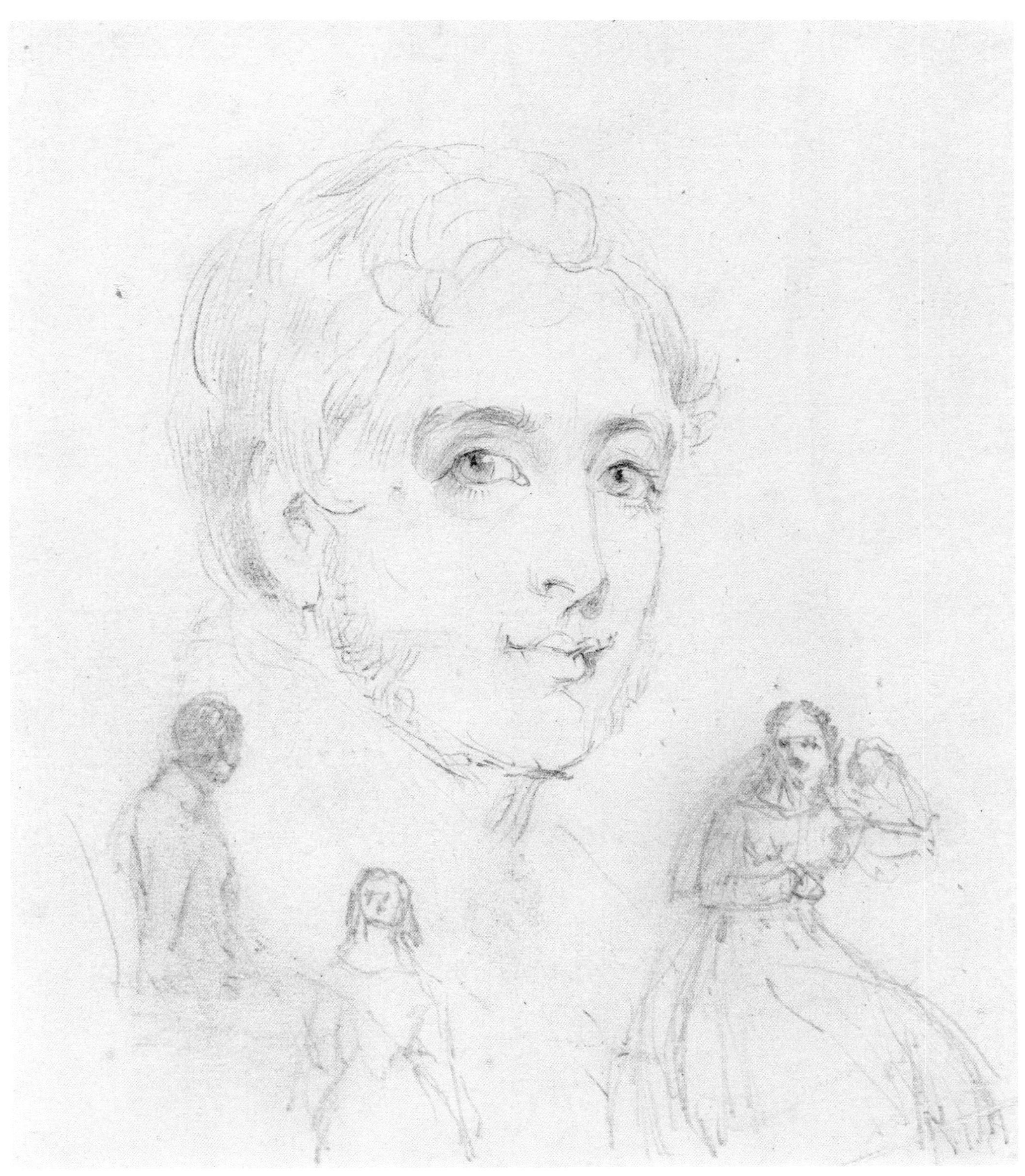

Study of a man's head, c. 1840s

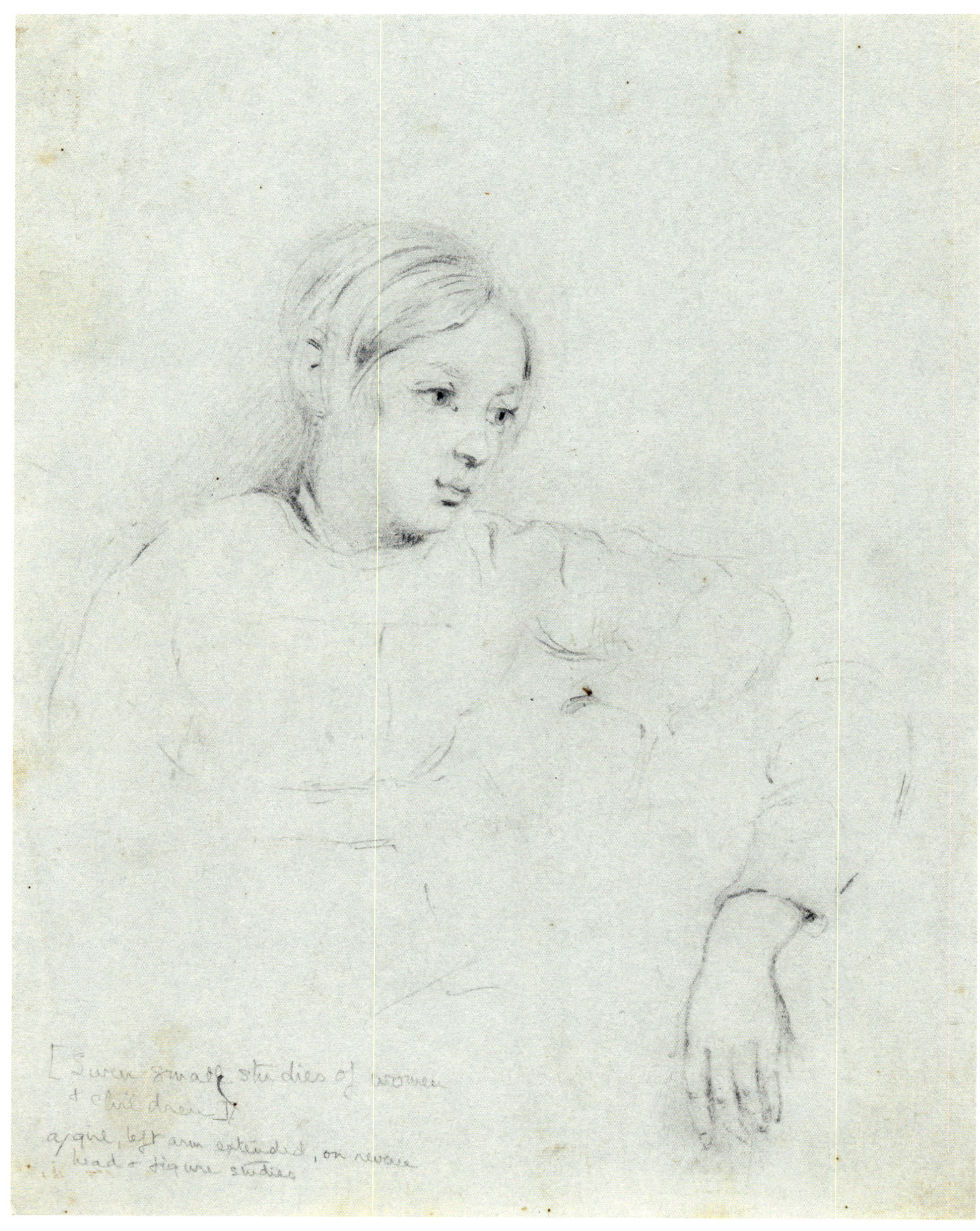

Girl with arm extended, c. 1830s

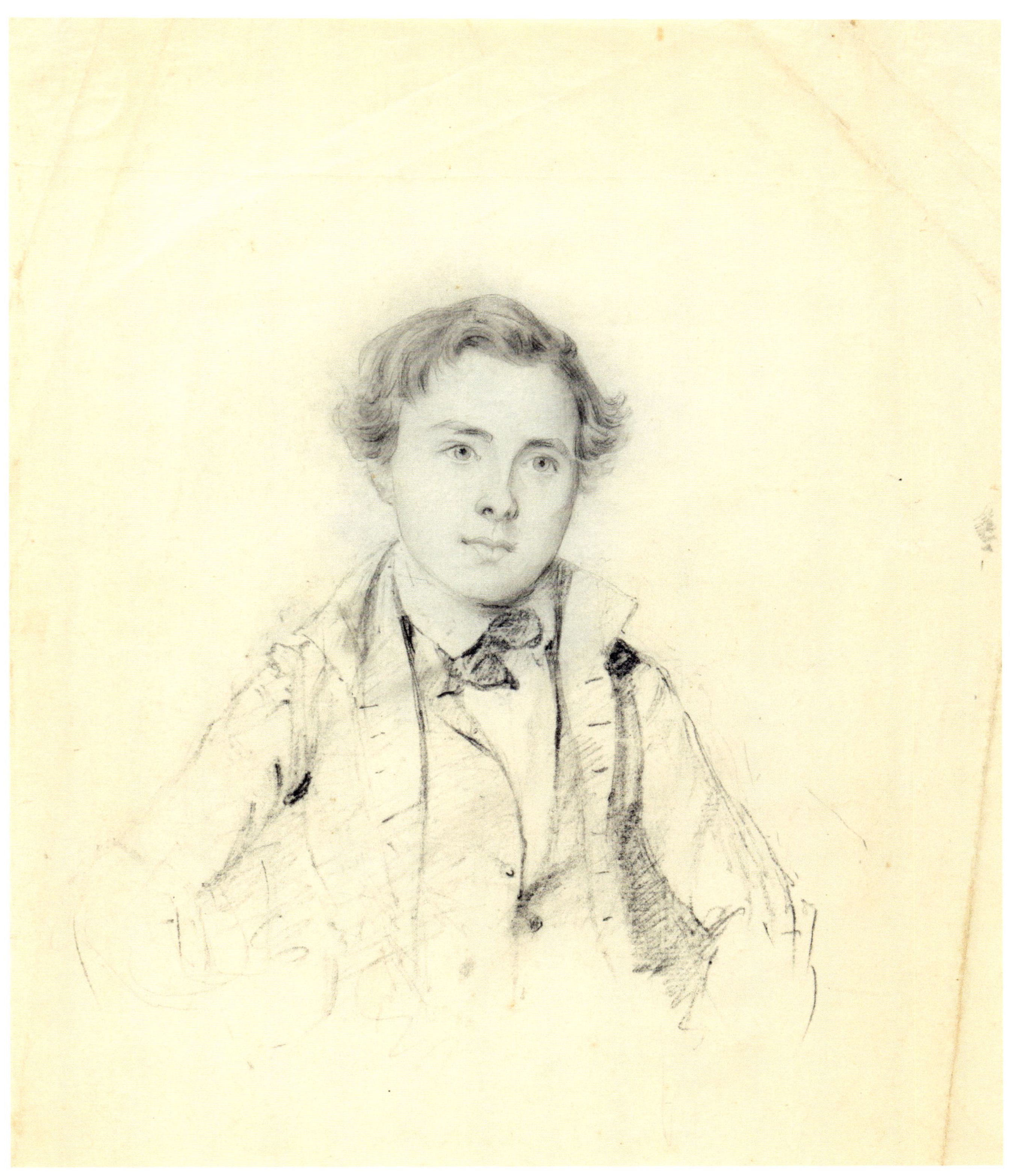

Half-length study, full face of a boy, c. 1830s

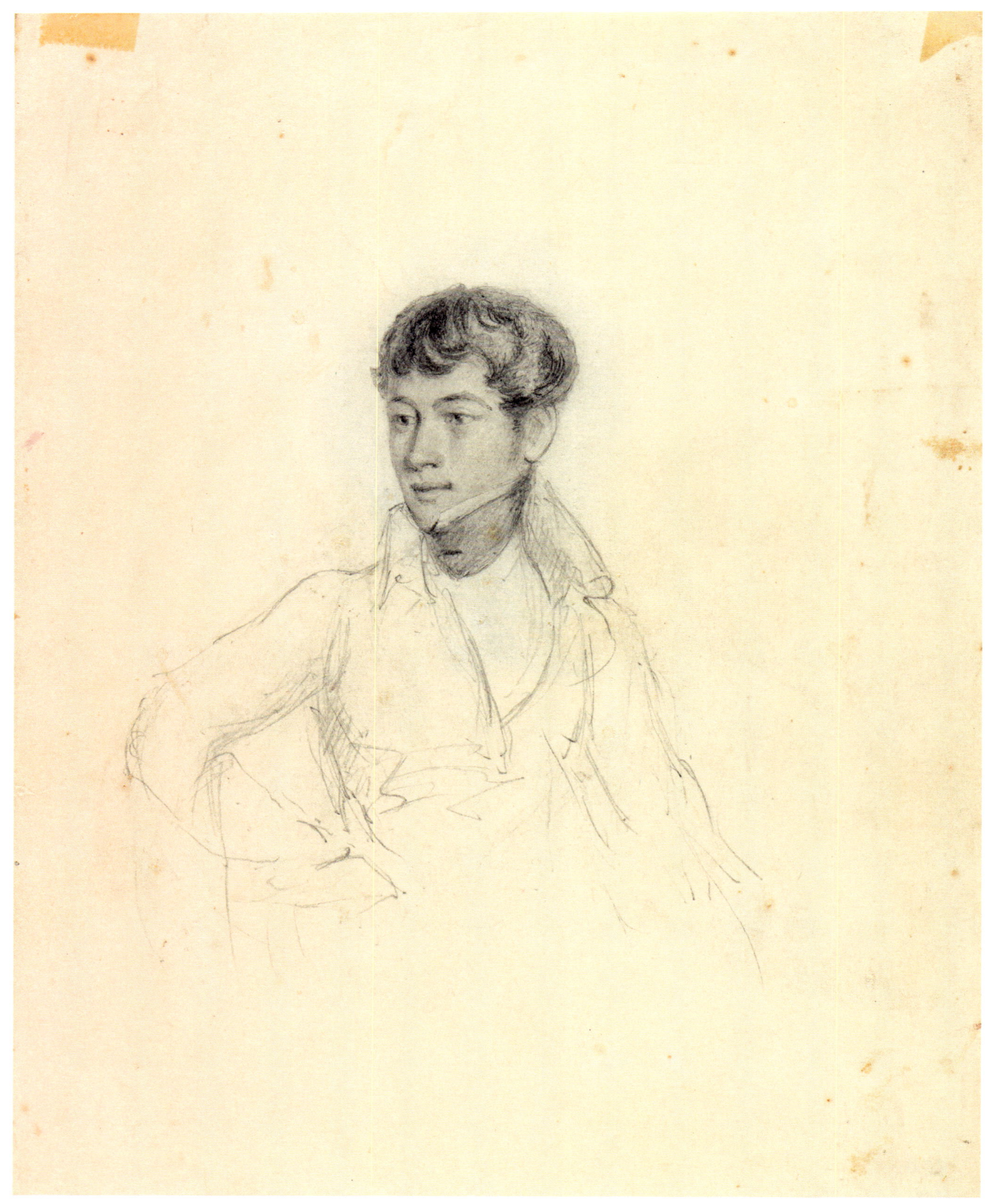

Half-length portrait of a young man, c. 1830s

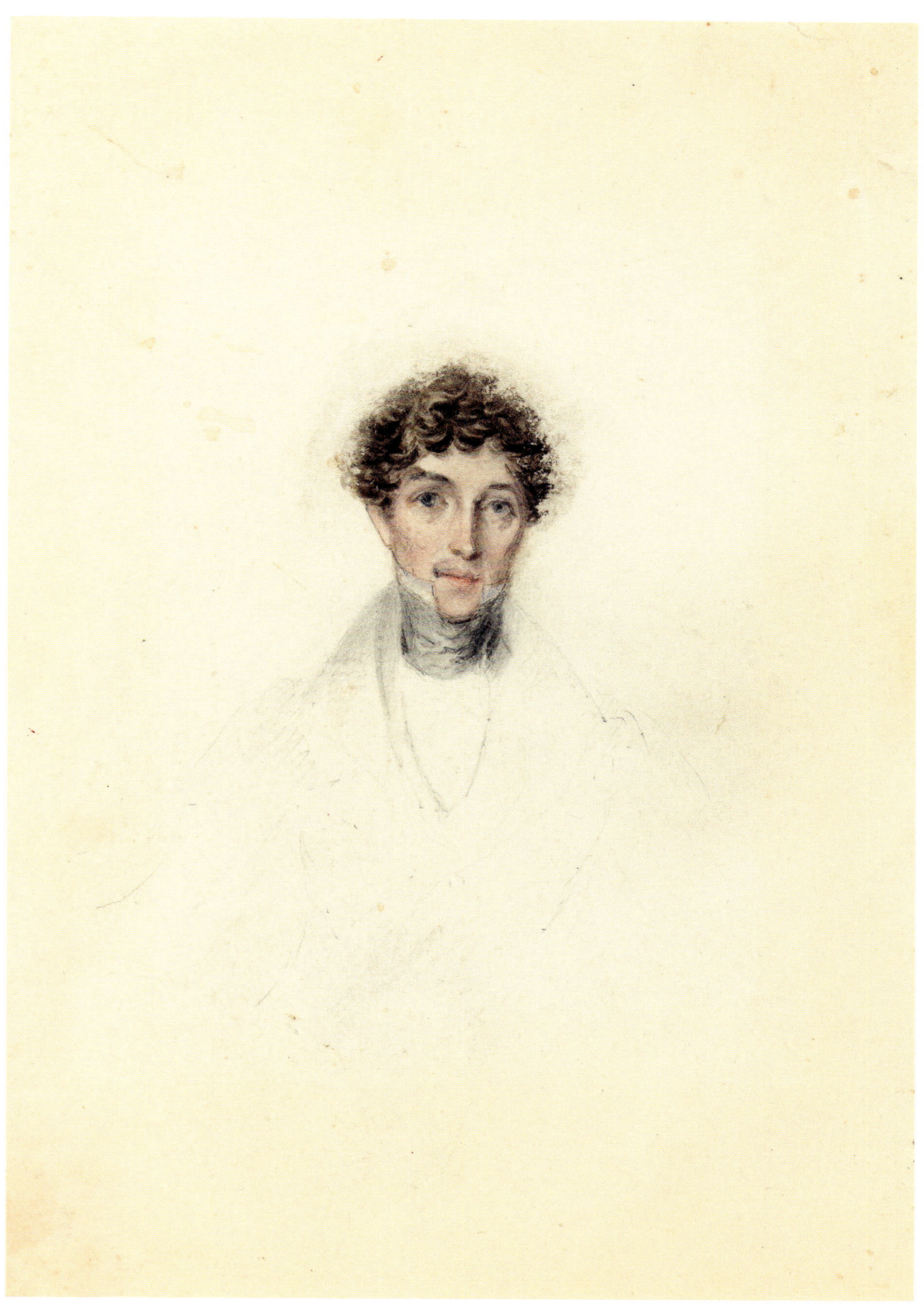

Head of a man. Heavily scored in tracing, c. 1830s

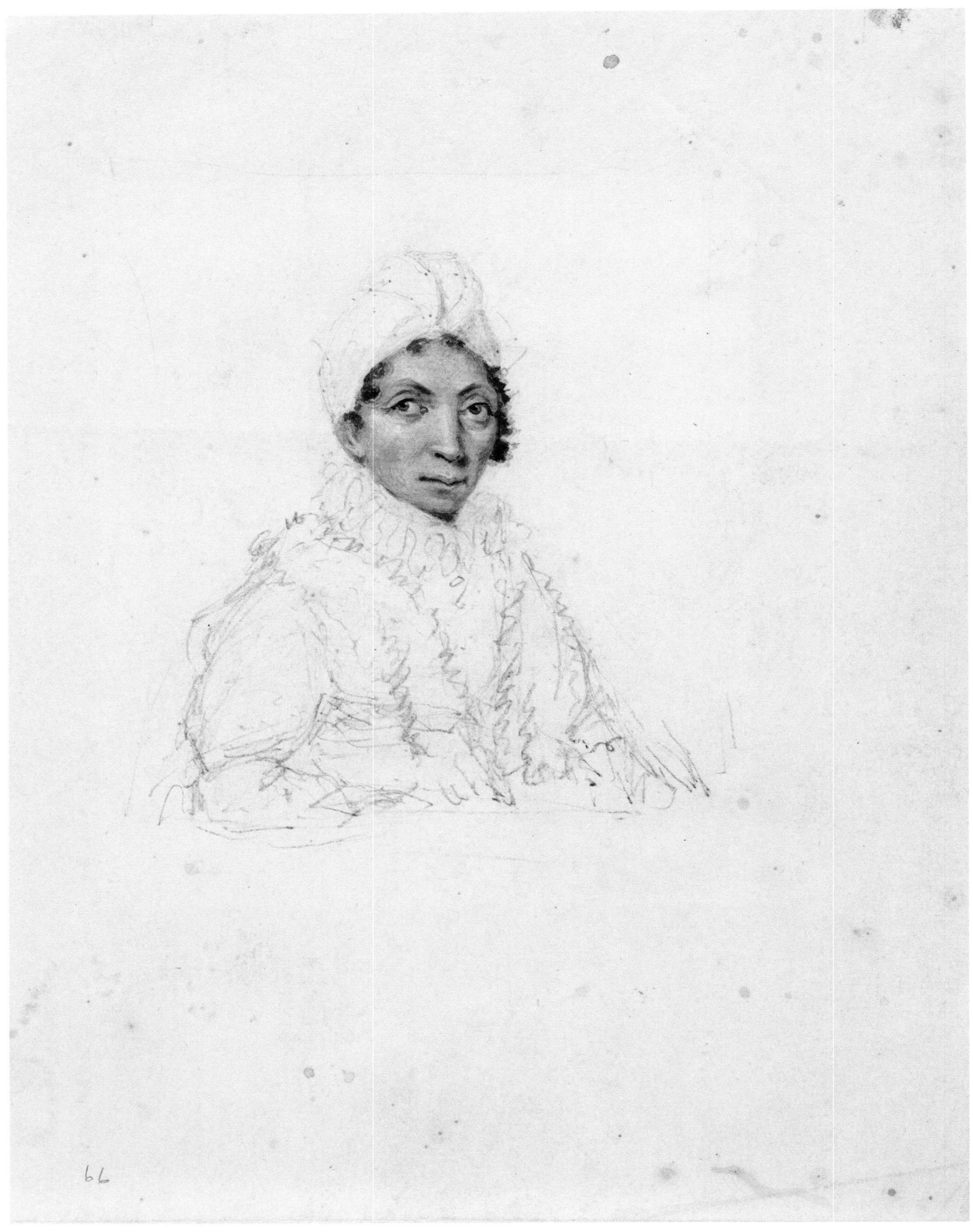

Woman with dark eyes, face finished with colour, c. 1830s

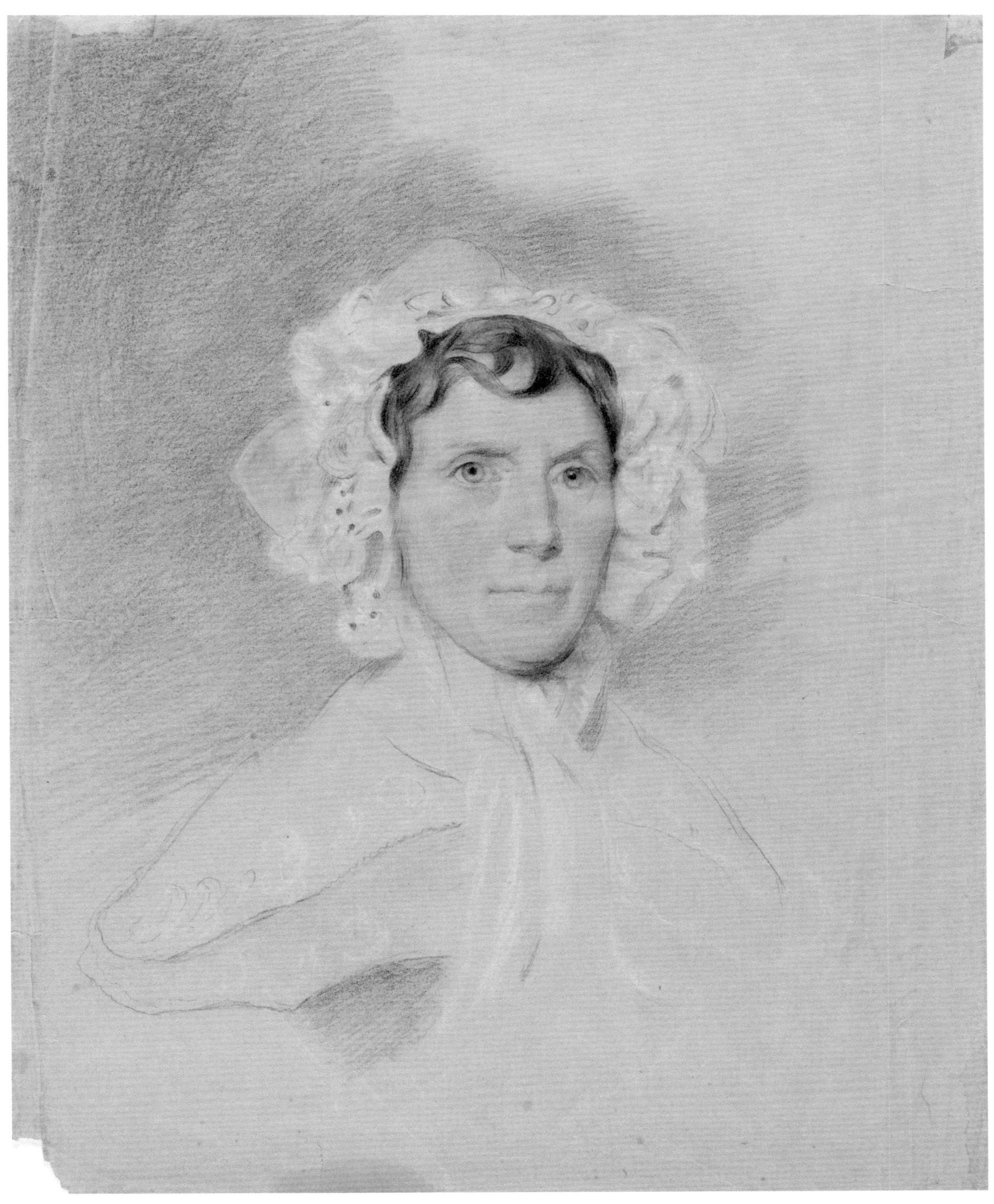

Half-length portrait of female figure in house cap, c. 1840s

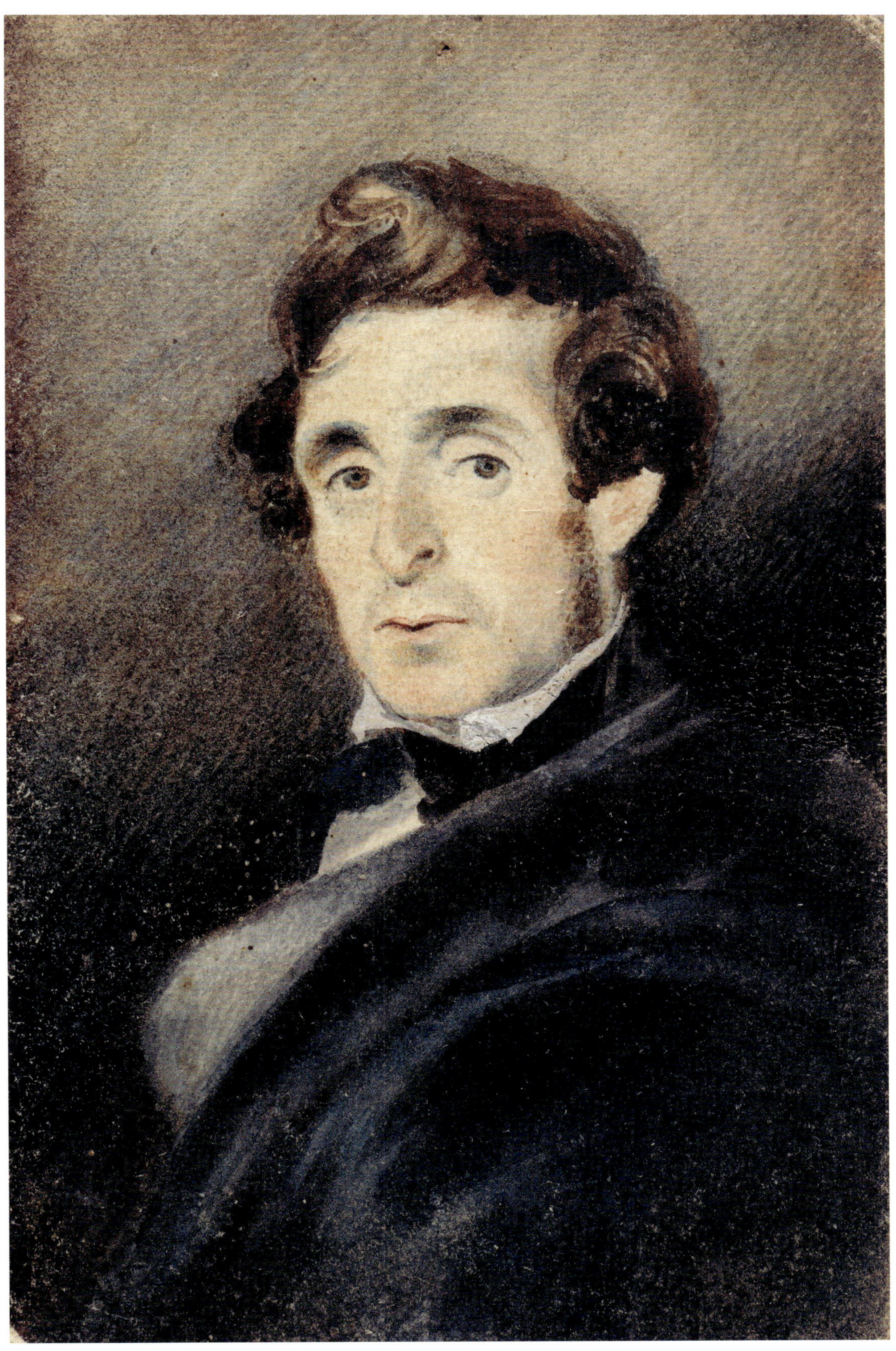

Portrait of William Buelow Gould, c. 1839

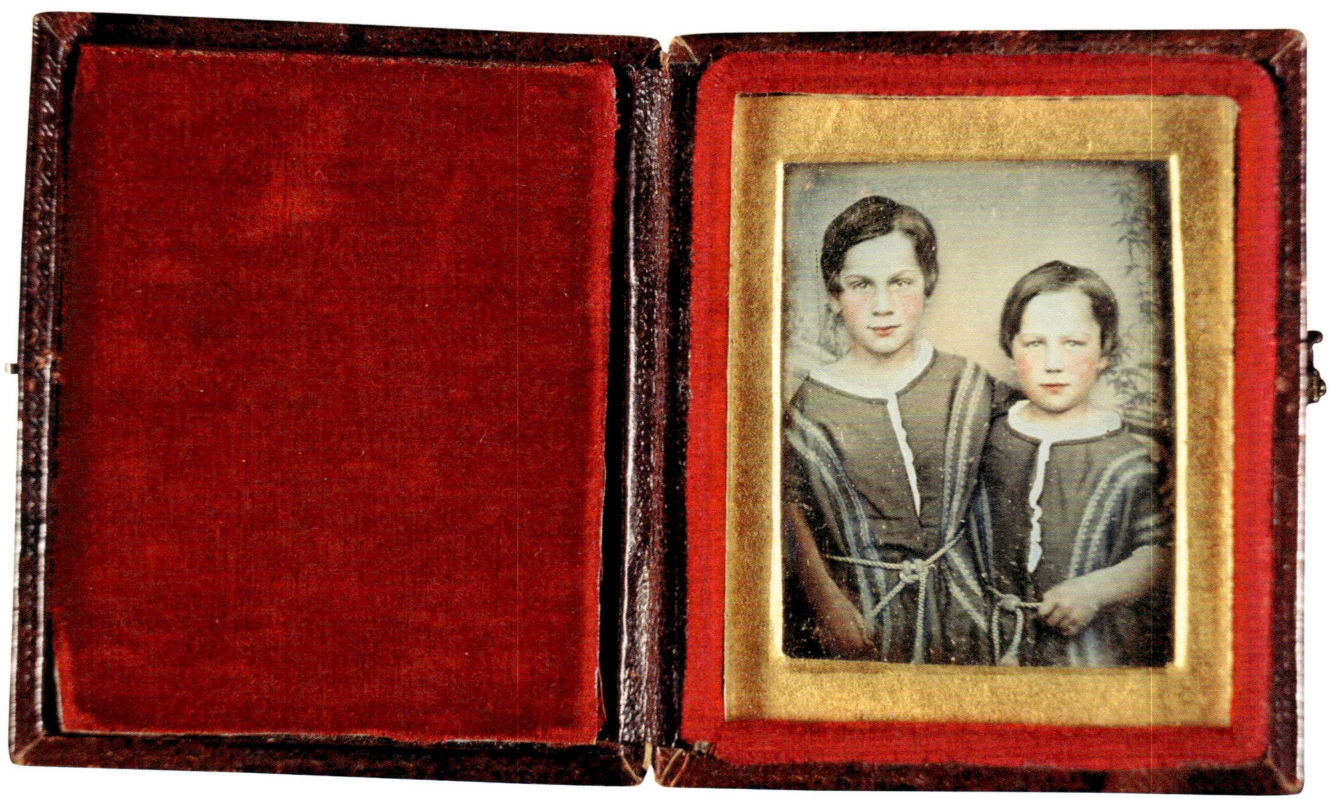

James and Henry Barnard, c. 1850

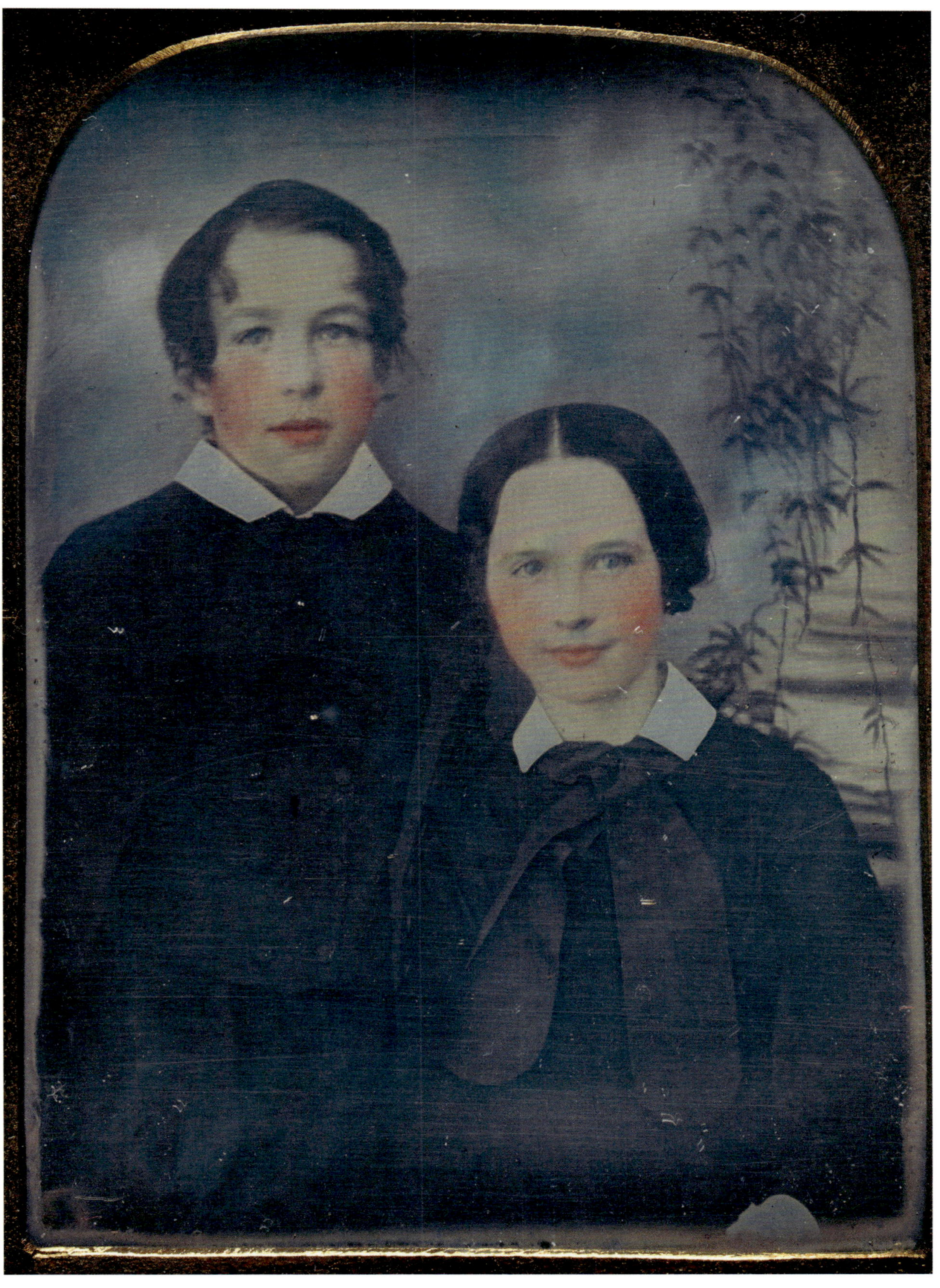

Two figures, possibly Downes and Charlotte Barnard, children of Tasmanian Government printer John Barnard, c. 1850

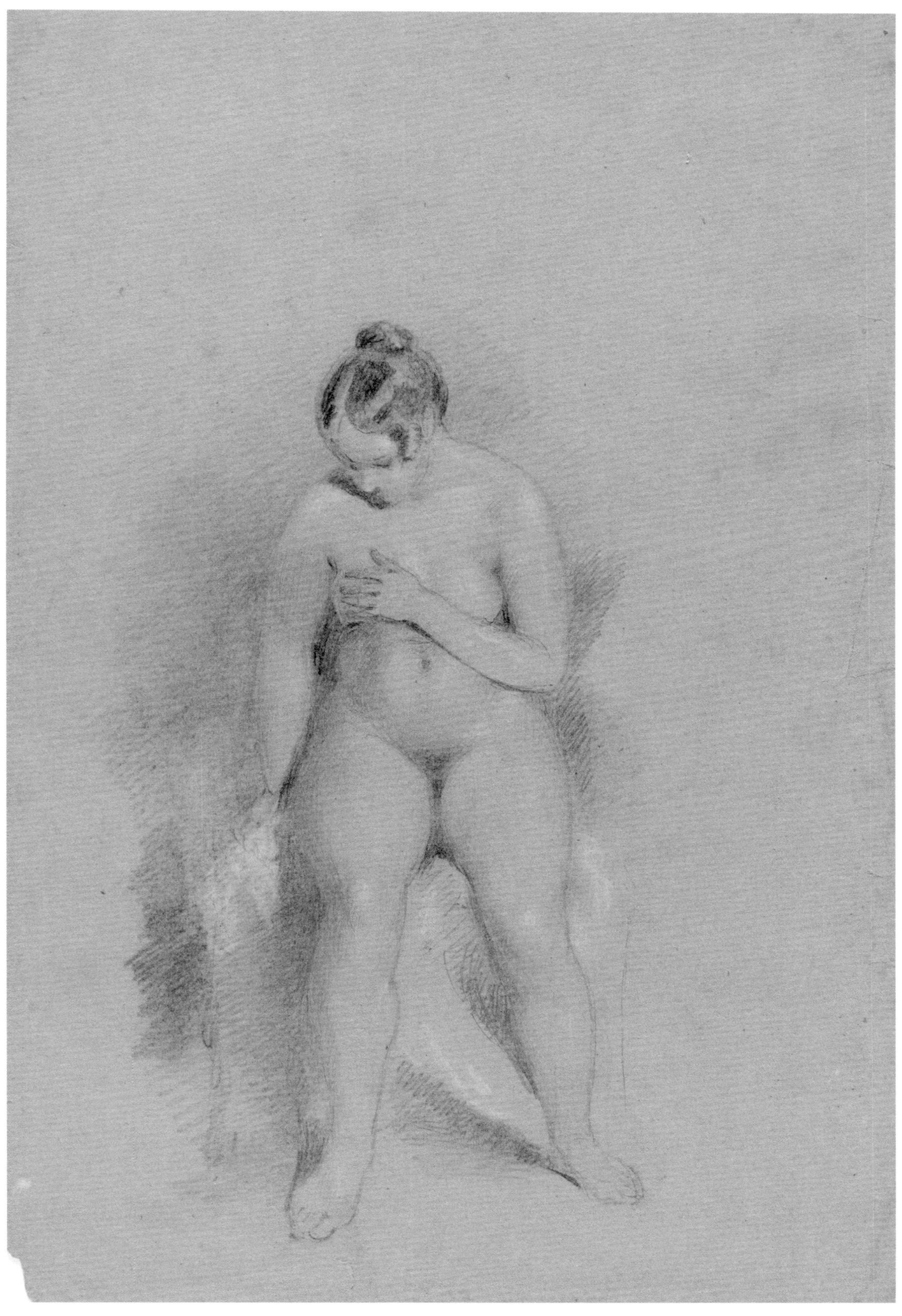

Seated female nude, c. 1840s

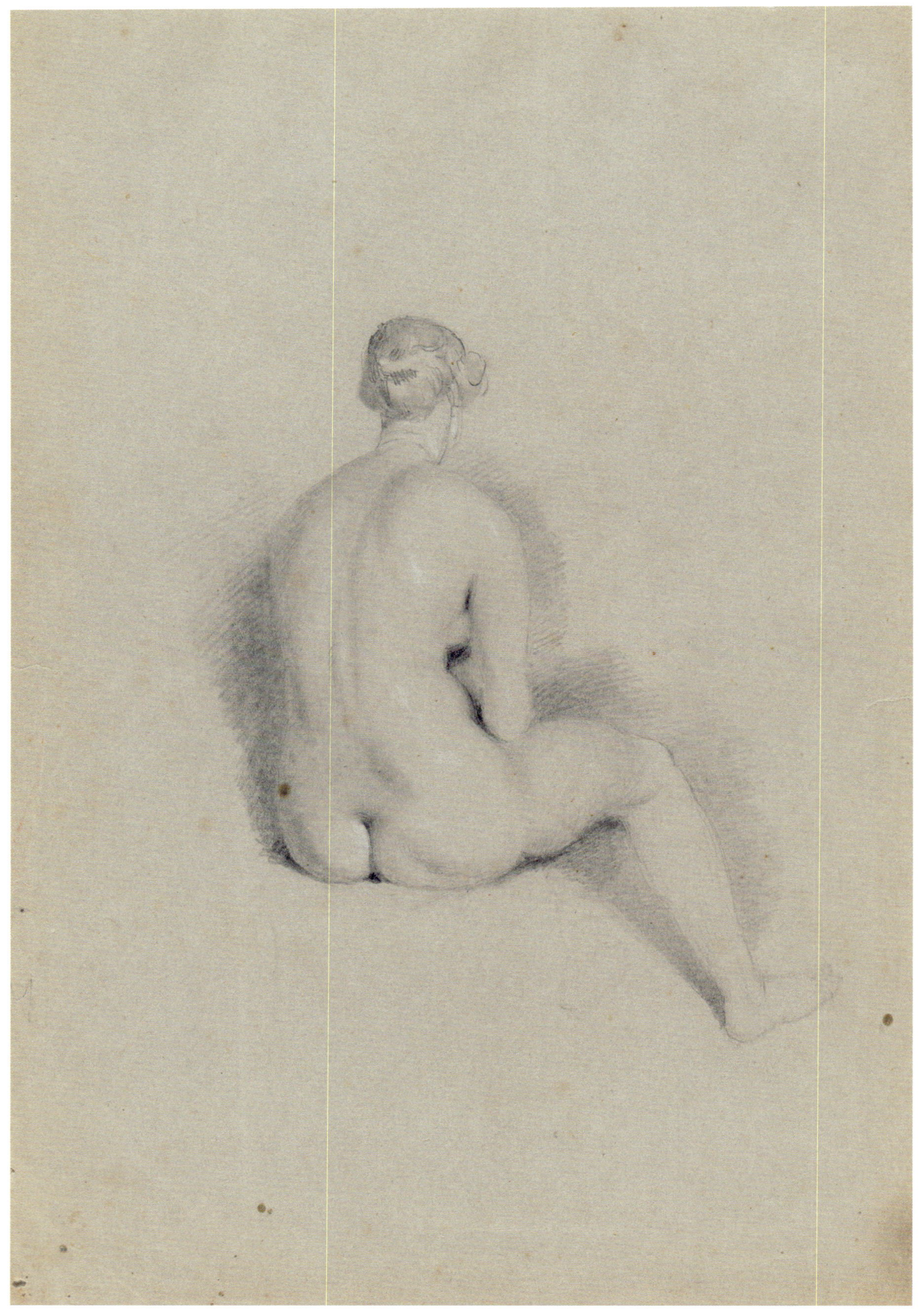

Seated female nude, back view, c. 1840s

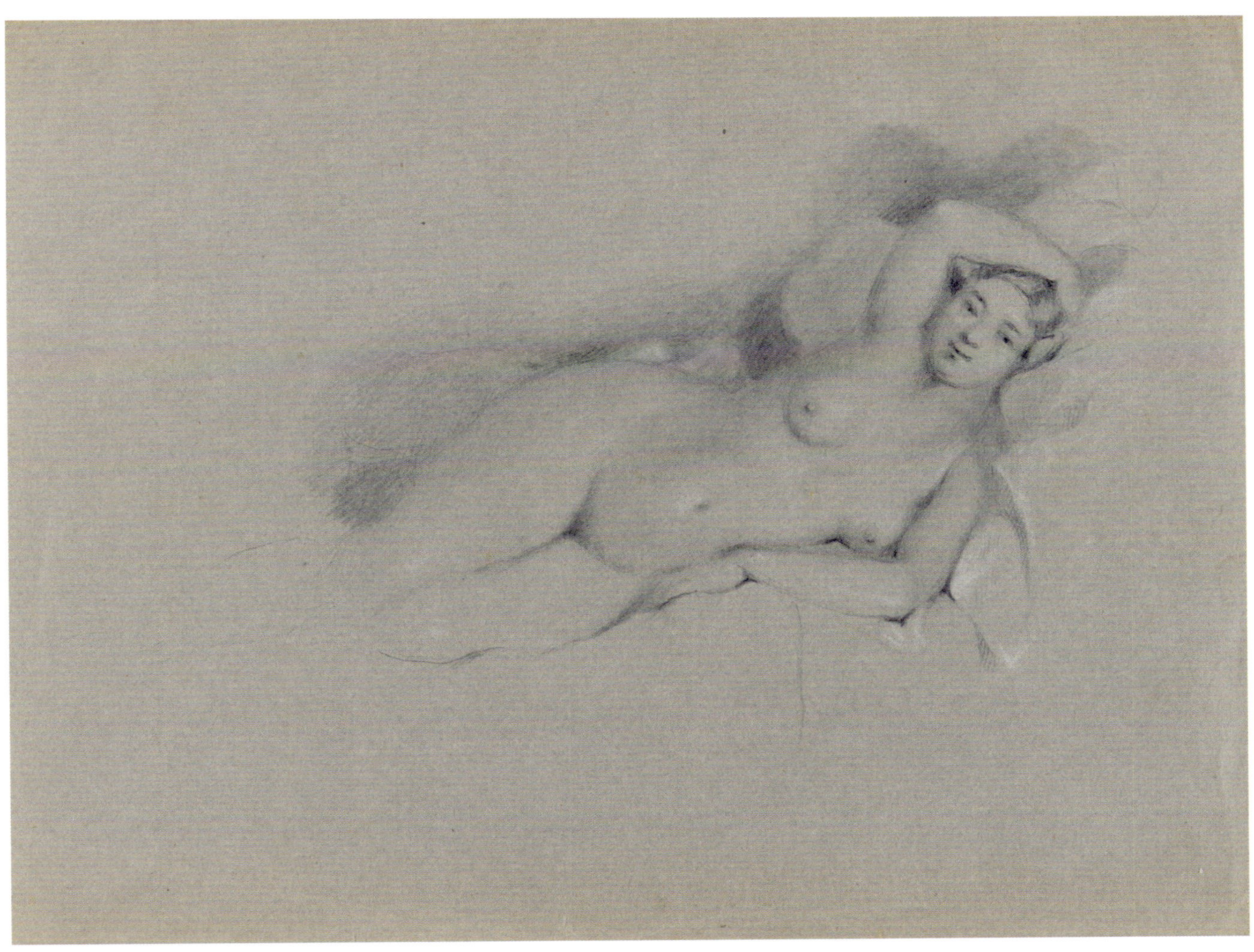

Reclining female nude, c. 1840s

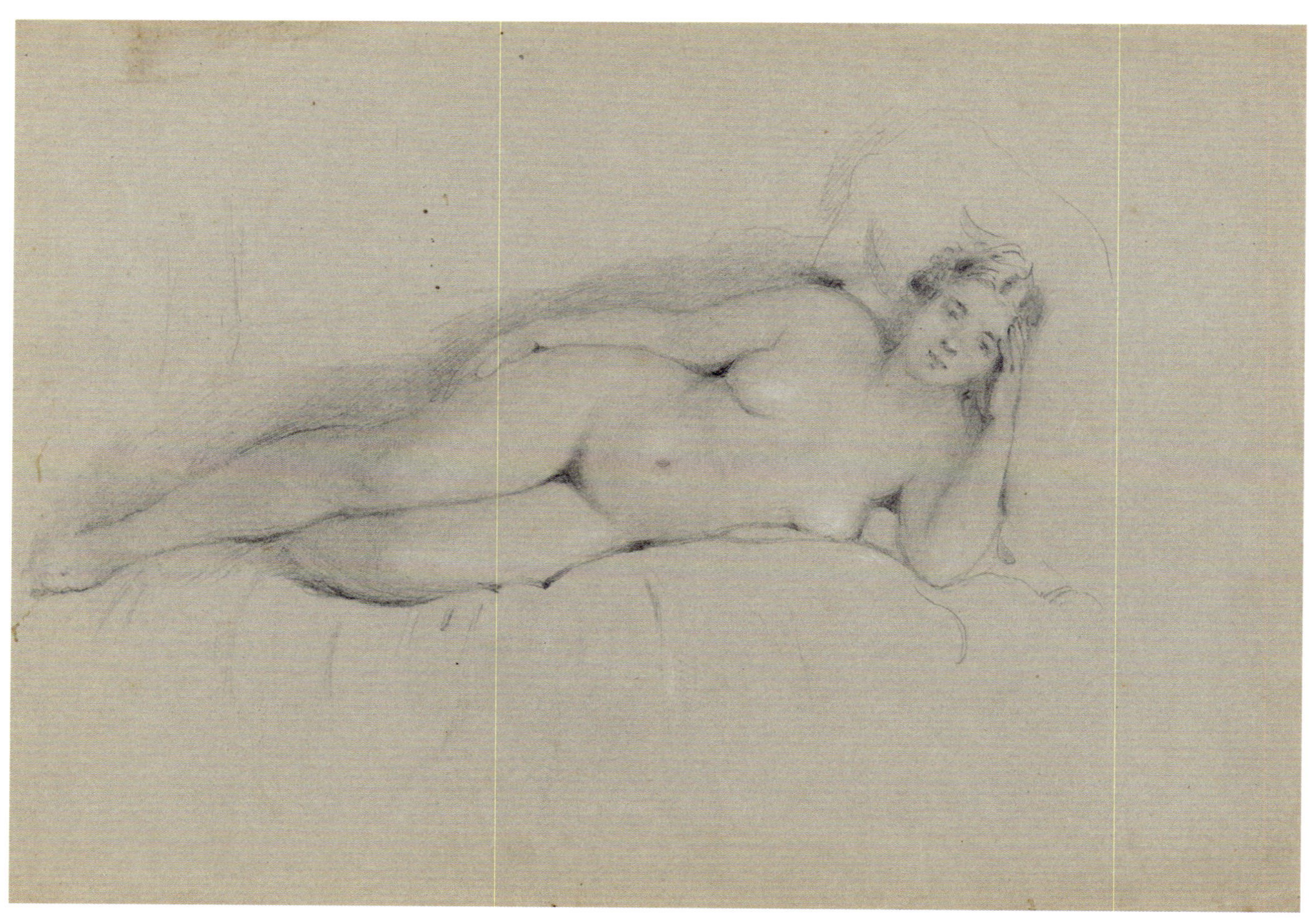

Reclining female nude, c. 1840s

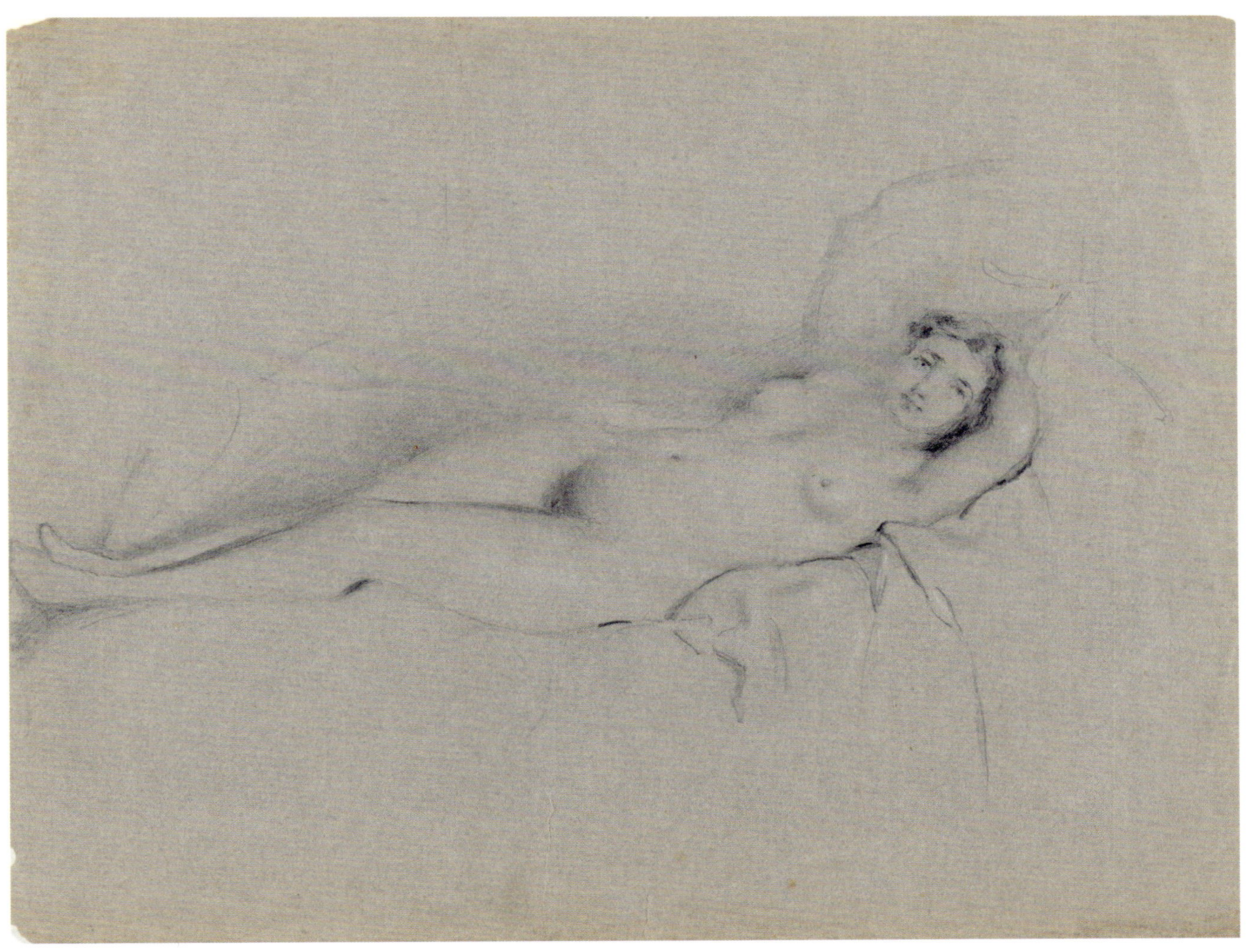

Reclining female nude, c. 1840s

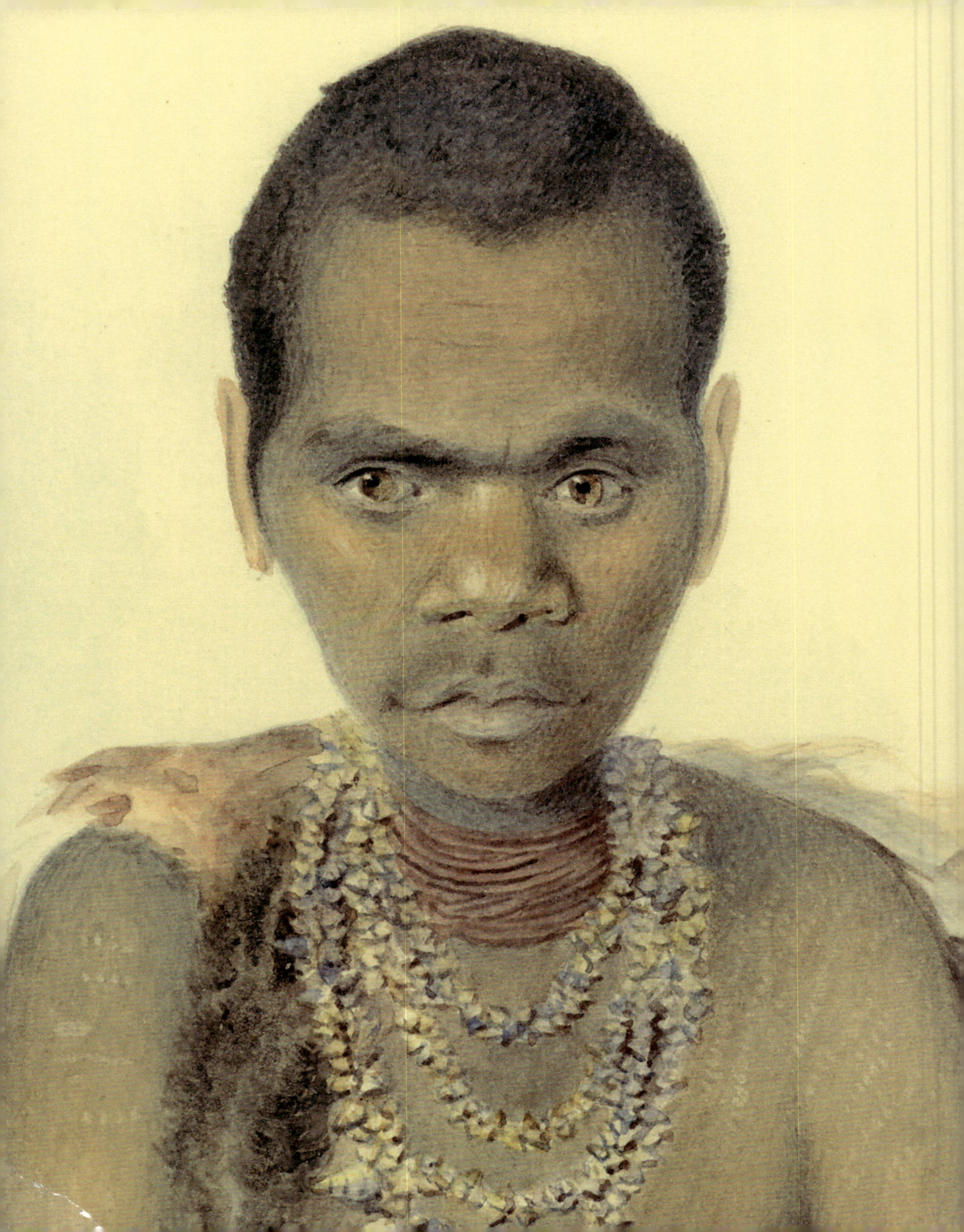

Thomas Bock and the mystery of Trukanini's shell necklace

Gaye Sculthorpe

Of the fourteen watercolour portraits of Tasmanian Aboriginal people by Thomas Bock, it is that of Trukanini[1] which is perhaps the best known and most reproduced. Apart from this work and the later portrait of Mithina (Mathinna), the portraits have been exhibited to date largely biography-free, in notable contrast to those of Bock's non-indigenous people of Hobart. This is despite several decades of community and historical interest and extensive research into the lives of Aboriginal people in colonial Tasmania. Commentators from the 1830s until the 1990s tended to regard these portraits as evidence of a people nearly extinct, while art historians have focused their attention on stylistic interpretation, with little regard for the lives of the people portrayed. While each portrait is worthy of individual consideration, despite past intense scrutiny, the study of even Trukanini's portrait can still be revealing.

For Aboriginal people in Tasmania today (*Palawa),* Bock's portraits of their ancestors and kin are significant cultural documents, giving cause for much reflection on their individual lives, the events they witnessed, and in which they were active participants. In brief, these men and women lived through a period of violent killings on the colonial frontier of Van Diemen's Land, and then fought in or survived a war waged against them. During and after a period of martial law, an immigrant bricklayer from London, George Augustus Robinson travelled through Tasmania from 1830 to 1834 with a small coterie of Aboriginal people on a "friendly mission" trying to conciliate other Aboriginal people at large and seeking to remove Aboriginal women living with sealers in conditions akin to slavery.

With Robinson's help, by 1835 the Aborigines were exiled to Flinders Island, under a dubious guise of government promise of protection, where most died.[2] Between 1839 and 1842, a number of Aborigines including Trukanini spent time with Robinson in the Port Phillip District (Victoria) where two men, Tunaminawayt and Malapuwinarana were publicly hanged after being convicted for killing two whalers.[3] In 1847, the 46 surviving Aborigines at Flinders Island were removed to Oyster Cove Aboriginal Station, south of Hobart where their numbers continued to decline, although some women remained with sealers on the islands of Bass Strait.

It is not surprising that Trukanini's portrait has received so much attention. As probably the best known Tasmanian Aboriginal person in history, she was widely but erroneously believed to be "the last Tasmanian" when she died in 1876. Born at Recherche Bay about 1812, Trukanini belonged to the Lyluequonny clan of the Southeast Nation. She played a key role in guiding Robinson on his expeditions around Tasmania, and, with others, accompanying him to Port Phillip.[4] Living through a time when Aboriginal human remains were in high demand from European anatomists and museums, and being aware of the scandalous post-humous mutilation of William Lanne, "the last Tasmanian man", Trukanini's fears for her own body were well-founded. The exhumation of her body after her death in 1876 and later display of her skeleton at the Tasmanian Museum and Art Gallery between 1905 and 1947 and its eventual return to the Tasmanian Aboriginal community for cremation in 1976 are part of the reason she remains legendary. In 1997 historian Lyndall Ryan noted that Trukanini was then the subject of "more than fifty poems, several histories and biographies, at least fifty paintings and photographs and nearly fifty scientific articles" as well as being the subject of a song, place names and represented on a postage stamp.[5]

Another reason Trukanini remains so widely known is because many colonial artists drew or fashioned her portrait: Robert Neill, Robert Dowling, Thomas Napier, Benjamin Dutterau, Benjamin Law, John Skinner Prout and Thomas Bock. She was also later much photographed.[6] As Bock's 1831 portrait is the earliest surviving portrayal,[7] it has been widely reproduced including in James Fenton's *The History of Tasmania* in 1884. Many commentators have written about the Bock portrait and other images of Trukanini, discussing her facial features, skin colour, likeness to other images, questions of accuracy of and symbolism of her representation as well as the distinctive shell necklaces she wore. Rebe Taylor says that looking at the face of Trukanini launches "an internal conversation" about the genocidal events in Tasmania's colonial past and queries if we still need to look at Trukanini to understand these.[8] Ray Norman states that "the potency of these shell necklaces famously worn by Truganini is palpable"[9] and, like Trukanini herself, being deeply engrained in Tasmania's memory. Andrys Onsman has speculated on the frequency of and reasons for the portrayal of Trukanini with a shell necklace, commenting "It's an item that is so closely identified with her that it almost seems to be a part of her".[10] Of Bock's portrait, he notes that she is portrayed noticeably devoid of shell necklaces by contrast with images of her done by Duterrau (and in later photographs).[11] Other writers such as Julie Gough and John Hawkins note also that is only Wutapuwitja (Wortabowigee) who Bock portrays wearing a shell necklace.[12]

Why might this be so? I argue that the reason why Bock's portrait of Trukanini shows her without a shell necklace is due to a nineteenth century historical error of identification: Bock's supposed portrait of "Truggernana", is not actually of her, but is of Wutapuwitja; and, conversely, Bock's "Wortabowigee", wearing a shell necklace, is really Trukanini. The evidence for this is outlined below.

Provenance of Bock's portraits of Tasmanian Aborigines

Thomas Bock created at least five and perhaps up to seven sets of Aboriginal portraits. The original set was commissioned by George Augustus Robinson and completed between October 1831 and September 1835, almost certainly as illustrations for a book he hoped to write. Bock later made copy sets of these portraits, probably based on a set of outline sketches: firstly for Jane, Lady Franklin in 1837 and then a set for the Rev. Henry Dowling in about 1838.[13] N.J.B. Plomley has researched these extensively and notes sets in the collections of the British Museum, the Pitt Rivers Museum, the Tasmanian Museum and Art Gallery (TMAG), the Alexander Turnbull Library, Wellington, and a set once in the Ethnological Society in London (now the Royal Anthropological Institute). The content of the sets differ. At the British Museum, TMAG and the Pitt Rivers Museum they consist of a core set of portraits (what Plomley calls the "popular" set) and five facial profiles done in blue. In addition, the British Museum has four unique portraits: that of Muntipiliyata (Montpelliater), Tanalipunya (Tanleboneyer), Multiyalakina (Eumarrah) and a portrait of a young man, possibly a Hawaiian.[14] TMAG has the only known portrait of Mithina (Mathinna), commissioned by Lady Franklin, c. 1842.

The original set of Bock's portraits is that in the collection of the British Museum. Robinson took this set back to Britain when he returned to live there in 1852. The year after his death in 1866, Robinson's widow sold these portraits, other pictorial works and artefacts collected by him to the Staffordshire surgeon and collector Dr Joseph Barnard Davis.[15] After Davis died in 1881, his large collection of books and pictures was auctioned in London, the Tasmanian portraits and other material then acquired by A.W. Franks for the British Museum.[16] The portraits auctioned were listed generically in groups; for example, Lot 32: "Eight Watercolour Drawings, 6 Portraits, Canoe and Group of Natives of Tasmania" which sold for ten shillings. In 1856, Barnard Davis had tried to buy the set of portraits owned by Lady Franklin without luck. He then commissioned G. Gray, "a friend, an excellent artist", to make a copy of the Bock portraits from the set purchased by the Ethnological Society of London in 1855.[17] Consequently, the British Museum has the fourteen watercolour portraits and five blue profiles by Bock together with the copies by Gray of seven of the portraits.

The history of the Pitt Rivers Museum set is not clear but they were on display in London by 1878.[18] In 1965, Plomley stated that these were clearly the set that belonged to the Franklins; however, in 1991, he referred to them as Bock's reference set. French phrenologist Pierre Dumoutier of the Dumont d'Urville expedition remarked on them when the expedition visited Hobart in 1839.[19] Plomley tentatively identifies the set at the Turnbull Library as the Lady Franklin set done in 1837.[20] The set now in TMAG (the Rev. Henry Dowling set) was copied from the set produced for Lady Franklin. Dowling used this set as the basis of his oil paintings done later of the same subjects.[21]

Error in naming and identification

None of the Bock portraits produced for Robinson between 1831 and 1835 were signed by the artist and only one has the name of sitter inscribed ("Togerlongerter"). These works are no longer in their original frames; however, the British Museum database has a record of

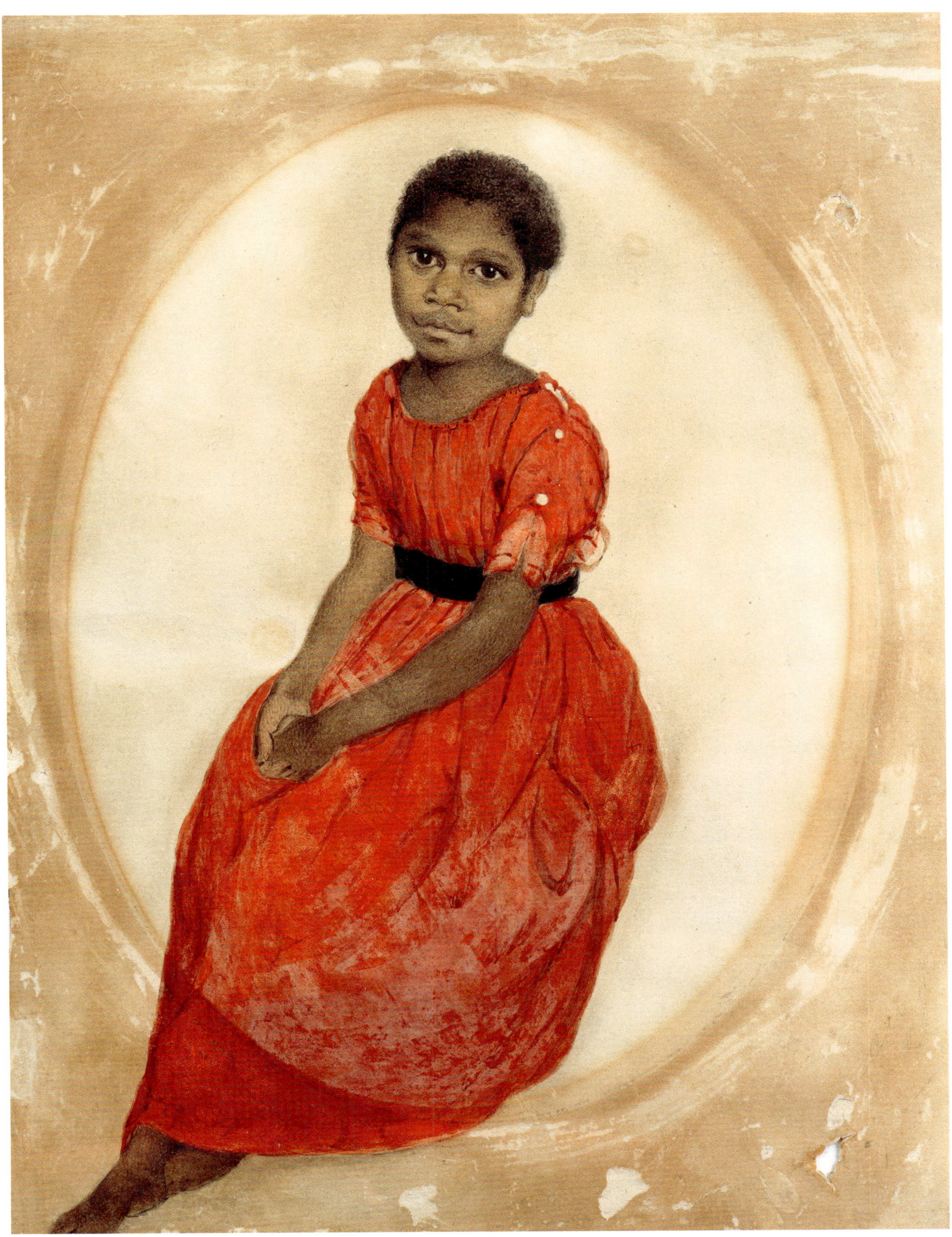

Mithina (Mathinna), 1842

what was written on these. This was not the names of the people portrayed but numbers from Davis's *Catalogue of Drawings, Pictures and objects of an Ethnological nature.*[22] All but two of the Bock portraits in the British Museum have a framed drawing number and for those which do, the number corresponds with the number in the Davis catalogue.[23]

Examination of the relevant Davis catalogue numbers and associated descriptions, the Bock drawings in the British Museum, and the record of catalogue numbers once on the frames evidences a significant error of transcription. The portrait currently named as *Wortabowigee* has a note "J B Davis Framed Drawing No. 5" and in the Davis Catalogue No. 5 is *Truggernana.*[24] Similarly, the portrait currently named as *Truggernana* has a note "J B Davis Framed Drawing No. 6" and in the Davis Catalogue No. 6 is *Wortabowigee.* The Davis catalogue descriptions of these portraits are as follows:

> 5. Fine coloured Drawing of "Truggernana" ♀ by Bock.
> Trugernanna presents the natural colour of the skin. I have no doubt she was a native of Bruné Isl. Shell necklace.
> 6. Fine coloured Drawing of "Wortabowigee". By Bock. Native of Port Dalrymple. Has kangaroo skin dress and wheals on the arm but is not ochred.

These descriptions clearly indicate that it is Trukanini who is portrayed wearing a shell necklace. The question of which portraits were "ochred" or not seems to refer to other portraits as both the above portraits show "the natural colour" or "not ochred" skin. Thus the skin colour of each portrait cannot be used to differentiate each person, and both portraits show weals on the arms. Further evidence to support misidentification is by way of pencil inscriptions by Davis on the bottom right hand corner of Gray's copies of these two portraits. On Gray's *Wortabowigee* Davis has written "This is 'Truggernana'"; and, on the bottom right corner of the Gray portrait of "Truggernana", Davis has written, "This is not the trusted Truggernana. It is Wortabowigee."

Looking at the names inscribed on other sets of the portraits does not help with identification as Bock probably created these using outline sketches.[25] The Pitt Rivers Museum set is unsigned and the style of the names inscribed of the sitters is inconsistent: the portrait of "Wortabowigee" has only a pencil inscription stating "Jack's wife",[26] whilst the portrait of "Truggernana" has a three line inscription "Truggernana Native of the Southern part of Van Diemen's Land". Plomley says the writing of "Jack's wife" is almost certainly that of Robinson and the lettering of *Truggernana* is of a style characteristic of Bock.[27]

The Pitt Rivers Museum set also has pencil inscriptions on the side or below each portrait which Plomley surmises likely summarise conversations between Bock and Robinson, such words as "risible", "loquacious", "petulant" and so on being typical Robinsonisms and the biographical detail only such as he would know.[28] Thus the portrait of "Trugernanna" has a pencil comment: "Lalla rookh, wife of Woureddi aged 27. Part good – saved Mr R's life at Arthur River, by pulling log/2 spars of wood across river on which Mr R was." The portrait of "Wortabowigee" entitled *Jack's wife*, has the comment at right, "Fanny – aged 30 well-disposed but rather petulant."

Plomley originally thought that the writer of the personal comments and biographical details might have been Robinson's clerk but later had doubts. There seems some similarity between these and the writing of Lady Franklin.[29] She did visit Robinson in Bath at the time of the 1864 meeting of the British Association for the Advancement of Science.[30] The Pitt Rivers Museum has Tasmanian Aboriginal objects collected by Sir John Franklin and Lady Franklin dated from 1843 so an association of the Franklins with some of the portraits at the Pitt Rivers Museum perhaps should not be ruled out. The Franklins also visited Flinders Island in January 1838 where they were hosted by Robinson, met the Aborigines, inspected their cottages and saw them dance.

Bock's signature is on the two relevant portraits in the Alexander Turnbull Library. If, as Plomley suggests, this is the Lady Franklin set, it must be the first copy set and hence could indicate the origin of the error. The Henry Dowling set at TMAG was copied from the Franklin set so is not an independent source of information in relation to these considerations.

Comparison with other early representations

While caution must be exercised in comparing images of different artists, or even later photographs, examination of other early visual representations of Trukanini also lends some support to an error of labelling and consequently raises queries as to the identity of the sitters in later works by other artists. A rather coarse, unsigned painting by Thomas Napier depicting Wurati and Trukanini sitting side by side done c. 1832 in the collection of TMAG shows Trukanini looking more similar in appearance to Bock's *Wortabowigee* than to his *Truggernana*, although rather older in appearance. Neither person wears any neck ornamentation in this

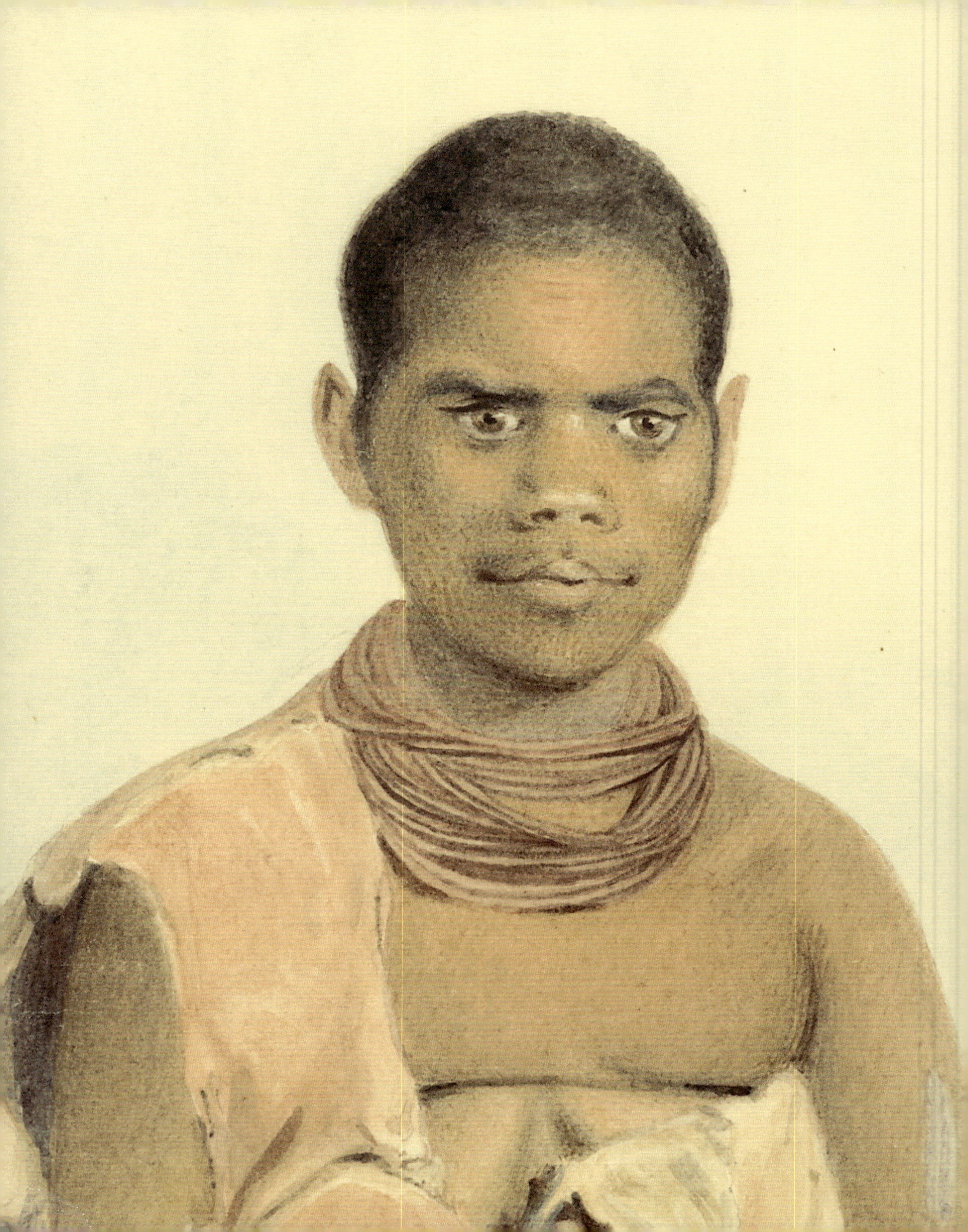

painting; however, the cicatrices portrayed on Trukanini also seem a closer match to that in Bock's portrait of Wutapuwitja.[31]

Benjamin Law sculpted a bust of Trukanini in 1836, about five years after Bock's portrait which shows her wearing a shell necklace.[32] As David Hansen has noted, at the time this bust, and another of Wurati, were made, they were considered "closely resembling nature"[33] and their production would have required "slow, careful scrutiny".[34] Mary Mackay has commented on the distinctive downcast gaze in this bust, suggesting this was sorrow for slain members of her family and race.[35] This slightly downward tilt of the head and the narrowing of the face seems more closely aligned to the portrait labelled to date as Bock's *Wortabowigee* (now *Trukanini* in my view) rather than to his *Truggernana*.

Benjamin Duterrau painted portraits in oils of Trukanini and three other Tasmanian Aborigines in Hobart in 1833. Bonyhady says of these works that they are "like all of Duterrau's art – unsuccessful as records of the Aborigines' clothing, physiognomy and skin colour".[36] Dutterau once commented that "painting, like poetry is not confined to strict historical truth"[37] and his portrait of Trukanini does not look like either of the two relevant sitters in Bock's portraits.[38] Geoffrey Dutton has even queried if it is in fact Trukanini in Dutterau's portrait, and suggested it was most likely Tanalipunya (Tanleboneyer).[39]

Nineteenth century historian James Bonwick recorded an observation of Trukanini told to him in 1832 by a lady who described her as being "exquisitely formed, with small and beautifully rounded breasts. The little dress she wore was loosely thrown around her person, but always with a grace and a coquettish love of display".[40] Onsman has commented that "Unfortunately there seems to be no record kept of the beauty or otherwise of the breasts of the woman who made the comment".[41] The oral account recalled by Bonwick clearly matches the description of Bock's *Wortabowigee* and it dates from the time of Bock's portraits. If we accept the misidentification, it shows Trukanini with rounded breasts and a loose kangaroo skin at her back, just as recollected. There are few descriptions and other representations available which can be used to compare the portrait of Wutawupitja.[42] The difference in age between the two women is perhaps only about three years and both appear with close cropped hair in Bock's portraits.

Questions arising

In considering the case for misidentification, several questions arise: could Barnard Davis have been wrong in his catalogue? Why did not Plomley notice this? If the handwriting on the portrait inscribed as *Jack's wife* (Wutapuwitja) at the Pitt Rivers Museum is by Robinson, could he have made a mistake? Would Bock have not known the difference between the two women? When and how could the error have occurred? I consider these issues briefly in turn.

Barnard Davis corresponded with Robinson from about 1862 and visited him in Bath that year. He recorded that Robinson had "12 Drawings of Tasmanians by Bock, which are in frames, and a few others not framed … Truggernana is not ochred."[43] In March 1867 he returned to Bath to buy Robinson's collection from his widow where he bought the drawings and other objects. In his descriptive pictorial catalogue dated 21 October 1867 he comments "shell necklace" in the description of *Truggernana* and he notes "This is not Truggernana" on the copy by Gray. Davis obviously had communication with Robinson and his widow, and given his definitive catalogue entries an error by him seems unlikely.

Assuming Plomley examined the copy portraits by Gray at the British Museum, the reason he may have missed the Davis pencil notations on these is that (today at least) the inscriptions cannot be seen unless one lifts the mount. Although Plomley had seen and copied the Davis catalogue which referred to Trukanini with a shell necklace, it is very easy to get confused with the differing numbers, lists and sets of portraits. I have looked at these portraits off and on over several years but not until I focused on the detail of these two portraits, added the Davis descriptive catalogue entries to the museum database, checked the inscriptions on the Bock and Gray works and the records from the old frames, did the misidentification become apparent.

If the inscription of "Jack's wife" on the Pitt Rivers portrait is in Robinson's hand, could he have made a mistake? Since he knew all the Aborigines well, particularly Trukanini, it might seem surprising. Yet Robinson often mixed up the labelling of objects in his collection confusing the artefacts from Tasmania and Victoria.[44] After speaking to Dr Joseph Milligan who had been the surgeon at Flinders Island and returned to live in England, Davis learnt how Robinson confused such matters and then wrote back to Mrs Robinson and asked her to buy back the collection he had bought as "it seems that all the objects I had from you are Australian and not Tasmanian, except the portraits".[45] Although Robinson knew a set of portraits was made for Lady Franklin,[46] he may not have seen them or the set done for

Dowling c. 1838 as he was only very briefly in Hobart in the period 1837–38 and from December 1839 to 1851 lived in Port Phillip.

I suggest Bock made the error, probably on either a reference set or the set made for Jane, Lady Franklin in 1837, due to his outline sketches seemingly being untitled and his not having seen the sitters for at least two years. In 1837 they were living, out of Bock's sight and out of mind, on Flinders Island and Robinson's original set, wherever it was, did not have titles or names of sitters recorded. With an error made only once, subsequent copies repeated it.

Conclusion

At least several commentators have expressed either a note of caution or puzzlement about portraits of Trukanini. Taylor refers to "presumably the lovely young woman in the 1837 Thomas Bock watercolour" and asks "but can we rely upon Bock's paintbrush to capture the 'real' Truganini, contained and self-reliant?"[47] Dutterau also portrayed Trukanini as part of the large group of Aborigines in his major painting *The Conciliation* in 1840.[48] As Taylor also notes, the identification of which individual in this painting is Trukanini has been the subject of much discussion over many years: is it the woman standing next to Robinson, the woman pulling Wurati, or the woman at the far back right hand corner peeking over the hill?[49] Stephen Scheding has queried if Trukanini really is the woman pointing at Robinson: "but is it really? ... She certainly looks like the woman in Thomas Bock's 1837 drawing of 'Trucanini' in the TMAG. Bock lived next door to Duterrau in Campbell Street, Hobart and Dutterau would have known Bock's portraits of her. But then, the woman leading Suspicion doesn't look like the person in Duterrau's known portraits of Trugernanna."[50] Hansen states that the Aboriginal people portrayed in Robert Dowling's *Aborigines of Tasmania* done in 1859 can be identified individually by comparing the figures to Bock's portraits as it were these images used in making copies for his father, the Rev. Henry Dowling.[51] If my argument is correct, Trukanini may thus be identified in error in this painting as well.

In comparing the portraits of Trukanini by Bock and Dutterau, Ryan has commented that Bock represented her "as vivacious and charming, a primitive with a 'noble countenance', the epitome of the 'noble savage'. By contrast, Benjamin Dutterau drew Trukanini as a strong, sturdy and stocky young woman, with bright eyes and a shaved head, wearing a shell necklace and with a possum skin flung over her shoulder. Here Trukanini is represented as a Pocahontas figure who saved the conciliator, G.A. Robinson, from the murderous intentions of the Tarkine people."[52] In 1833, the *Hobart Town Courier* described Trukanini's portrait by Dutterau as the "very picture of good humour"[53] whilst the *Trumpeter General* commented that although struck with the likenesses of Dutterau's Aboriginal portraits, the "merits of these having been shewn in vivid colours by a very able contemporary we abstain from further remark".[54]

Perhaps commentators from the 1830s until today have preferred to see a more lively and happy image of Trukanini rather than the more stern or sorrowful image in the other portrait, a reason Plomley suggests for Bock having omitted some portraits from his popular series.[55] Trukanini certainly had many things to be sad about, having witnessed atrocities against her close kin: her mother shot, sisters abducted by sealers and fiancé mutilated as well as her way of life completely transformed and later fearing that her own body would be abused after her death.

Despite the numerous interrogations and interpretations of the image of Trukanini, the mislabelling of Bock's portrait has misled investigators to date in this endeavour. In discussing Law's busts of Trukanini and Wurati, Hansen has emphasised the importance of uncovering "the material and documentary truths" of the lives of Aboriginal people and careful scrutiny of demonstrable empirical truths.[56] The mystery of Bock's portrait of Trukanini was revealed only by close physical inspection of the original works by Bock and the copies by Gray, by careful reading of Davis's catalogue noting a shell necklace and the documentation from the original frames. This highlights the importance of questioning commonly accepted "facts". Any study relying only on later sets of Bock's portraits such as the TMAG set would not have brought this information to light.

Now this error has been publicly exposed, we now need to look again with different eyes and consider all these associated issues anew. I think Trukanini would have been pleased that despite such intense visual and historical investigation to date, she has escaped being "captured" so easily by white men's eyes and European interpretations. Wearing both a fibre or sinew ochred necklace as well as a shell necklace and her face fixed with a stern gaze, Bock's portrait of Trukanini evokes the ongoing legacy of the events she witnessed which remain unreconciled in Tasmania today.

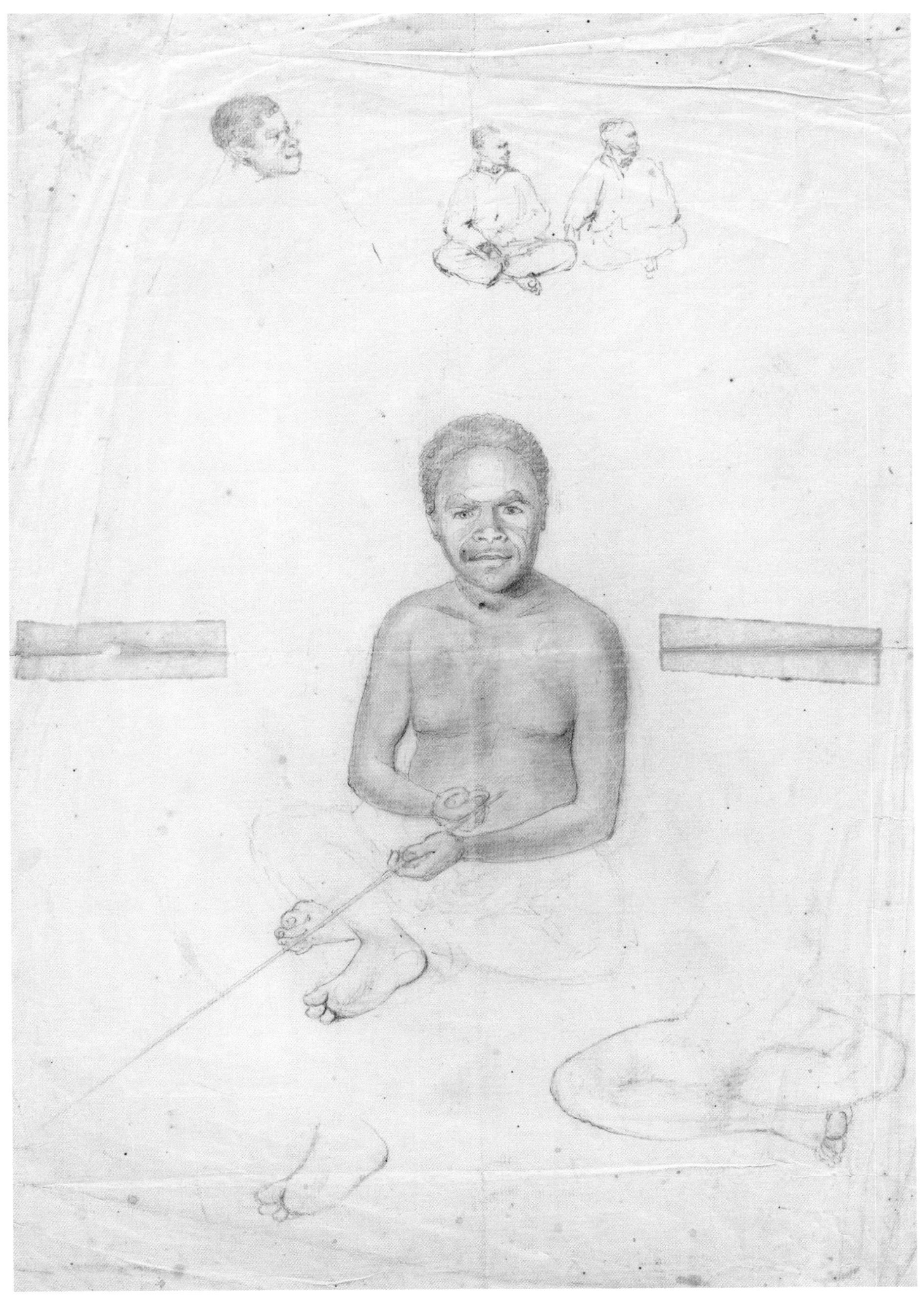

Unknown man holding a spear, early 1830s

1
For names of Aboriginal people, this article uses the spelling in *palawa kani*, the reconstructed Aboriginal language of Tasmania. The name Trukanini has been spelt many different ways in the past.

2
For a general historical account of these events, see Lyndall Ryan, *Tasmanian Aborigines. A History since 1803*, Allen & Unwin, Sydney 2012.

3
See Kate Auty and Lynette Russell, *Hunt Them Hang Them. 'The Tasmanians' in Port Phillip 1841–42*, Justice Press, Burwood 2016.

4
See Allison Cadzow, 'Guided by her: Aboriginal women's participation in Australian expeditions', Tiffany Shellam, Maria Nugent, Shino Kinoshi and Allison Cadzow (eds), *Brokers and Boundaries. Colonial Exploration in Indigenous Territory*, ANU Press, Canberra 2016, pp.85–118; Cassandra Pybus, 'Journey through the apocalypse. Ria Warrah, Wooreddy and Truganini', *Griffith Review* 58 2017.

5
Lyndall Ryan, 'The Struggle for Trukanini 1830–77', Peter Eldershaw Memorial Lecture, *Tasmanian Historical Research Association, Papers and Proceedings,* 44(3), 1977, p.153.

6
Photographers included Bishop Nixon, Alfred Woolley, C. A. Woolley, Henry Frith, Henry Hall Bailey and Samuel Clifford. The portrait by Neill has not been located.

7
For production dates, I rely on N.J.B. Plomley 'Thomas Bock's Portraits of the Tasmanian Aborigines', Diane Dunbar (ed.), *Thomas Bock. Society Portraitist, Convict Engraver*, exhibition catalogue, Victoria Museum and Art Gallery Australian National Gallery, Launceston and Canberra 1991, pp.33–41.

8
Rebe Taylor, 'The National Confessional', *Meanjin Quarterly,* 3, 2012, p.22.

9
Ray Norman, 'Necklaces and Placedness in Tasmania', *Coolabah,* 11, Observatori: Centre d'Estudis Australians, Australian Studies Centre, Universitat de Barcelona, Barcelona 2013), p.292.

10
Andrys Onsman, *How Tasmanian Aboriginals have been portrayed by White Australians: a history of racial and cultural deligitimization and the case of Truganini's necklace*, Edwin Mellen Press, Lewiston 2014, pp.149–50.

11
Ibid., p.196.

12
Julie Gough, 'Colonial Representation and Appropriation of the Tasmanian Aboriginal Shell Necklace', *kanalaritja. An Unbroken String*, exhibition catalogue, Tasmanian Museum & Art Gallery, Tasmanian Museum and Art Gallery, Hobart 2016, p.67; John Hawkins, 'A suggested history of Tasmanian kangaroo skin or sinew, human bone, shell, apple seed and wombat claw necklaces', *Australiana*, February 2008, p.26.

13
For further details see N.J.B. Plomley, 'Tasmanian Aboriginal Material in Collections in Europe', *Journal of the Royal Anthropological Institute of Great Britain and Ireland*, 91(2), 1961, pp.221–27; N.J.B. Plomley, 'Thomas Bock's portraits of the Tasmanian Aborigines', *Records of the Queen Victoria Museum Launceston,* New Series 18, 1965, pp.1–25; N.J.B. Plomley, 'Thomas Bock's portraits of the Tasmanian Aborigines', 1991, op. cit.

14
Joseph McLaine, or "John McLean", a Hawaiian seaman, was transported as a convict to Van Diemen's Land in 1828 and worked as a servant for G.A. Robinson during his travels. See N.J.B. Plomley (ed.), *Friendly Mission, The Tasmanian Journals and Papers of George Augustus Robinson* 1829–34, Queen Victoria Museum & Art Gallery & Quintus Publishing, Launceston 2008), p.621.

15
See Vivienne Rae Ellis, *Black Robinson. Protector of Aborigines*, Melbourne University Press, Melbourne 1998, pp.262–65.

16
Sotheby, Wilkinson & Hodge, *Catalogue of Decorative Porcelain, Antiquities & other Works of Art including the collections of the late Dr J. Barnard Davis ... on Friday, the 19th day of January, 1883,* Sotheby, Wilkinson & Hodge, London 1883, p.5. See also letter from A.W. Franks [unsigned] to Mrs Davis 14/2/1883, in "pre-1896" correspondence box D, Department of Britain, Prehistory and Europe, British Museum.

17
N.J.B. Plomley, 'Thomas Bock's portraits of the Tasmanian Aborigines', 1965, op. cit., p.20.

18
See Pitt Rivers Museum Online Object Catalogue for full details of each portrait: search for object 2008.77.

19
N.J.B. Plomley, 'Thomas Bock's portraits of the Tasmanian Aborigines', 1991, op. cit., p.41.

20
The records of the Turnbull Library set are not clear, but some of Bock's descendants such as Mrs J. H. Clark did live in Wellington and could possibly have been the source. They did present the "Mathinna" portrait to TMAG in 1951.

21
See John Jones, *Robert Dowling: Tasmanian son of Empire.* National Gallery of Australia, Canberra 2012.

22
Joseph Barnard Davis, Catalogue of Drawings, Paintings, and other objects of an ethnological nature, MS145, Royal Anthropological Institute, London 1867.

23
The two portraits that don't have numbers recorded were not in frames. Plomley refers to these as "Unknown A" (Tanleboneyer) and "Togerlongerter".

24
The British Museum registration numbers are Oc.2006, Drg 56 (*Wortabowigee*) and Oc. 2006, Drg 58 (*Truggernana*).

25
N.J.B. Plomley, 'Thomas Bock's portraits of the Tasmanian Aborigines', 1991, op. cit., p.41.

26
Like many Aboriginal people at that time, Wutaputwitja had several names assigned over her life time: Fanny, Jack's wife and Planobeena.

27
For details of the different styles of transcriptions, see N.J.B. Plomley, 'Thomas Bock's portraits of the Tasmanian Aborigines', 1965, op. cit.

28
Ibid. p.3; N.J.B. Plomley, 'Thomas Bock's portraits of the Tasmanian Aborigines', 1991, op. cit., p.37.

29
See sample of handwriting on letter at UTAS from Lady Franklin to Miss Hayter, n.d., http://eprints.utas.edu.au/8434/2/rs18_4_%282%29_letter_from_Jane_Franklin.pdf

30
Rae Elllis, *Black Robinson*, op. cit. p.260.

31
Tasmanian Museum and Art Gallery registration number AG3427.

32
See image online at https://www.portrait.gov.au//people/benjamin-law-1807

33
Hobart Town Courier, 7 October 1836, p.2.

34
David Hansen, 'Seeing Truganini', *Australian Book Review*, May 2010, p.50.

35
Mary Mackay, cited in Stephen Scheding, *The National Picture*, Random House, Sydney 2002, p.113.

36
Bonyhady notes these were done in 1833 but dated 1834. See Tim Bonyhady, 'To Quit the Barbarous for a Civilised Life: Benjamin Duterrau, The Conciliation, 1840', Daniel Thomas (ed.), *Creating Australia: 200 Years of Art 1788–1988*, International Cultural Corporation of Australia and the Art Gallery of South Australia, Adelaide 1988, p.76.

37
Benjamin Dutterau, Lecture at Mechanics Institute Hobart, 1849, cited in P. Paffen, 'A grand illusion: Benjamin Duterrau and *The Conciliation*', *Melbourne Art Journal*, 5, 1991, p.55.

38
See image online at http://catalogue.nla.gov.au/Record/1864707

39
Vivienne Rae Ellis, *Trucanini, Queen or Traitor?* Australian Institute of Aboriginal Studies, Canberra 1988, footnote 69, p.180.

40
James Bonwick, *The Last of the Tasmanians*, Low, London 1870, p.217.

41
Andrys Onsman, op. cit., p.75.

42
A caricatured image was created by Charles Brown Hardwicke when she was about eleven.

43
J. Barnard Davis, Notae Ethnographica, MS147, Royal Anthropological Institute, London.

44
See Gaye Sculthorpe, 'The Ethnographic Collection of George Augustus Robinson', *Memoirs of the Museum of Anthropology and History, Memoirs of the Museum of Anthropology and History,* 1 (1), 1990, pp.1–96.

45
Vivienne Rae Ellis, *Trucanini, Queen or Traitor*, Australian Institute of Aboriginal Studies, Canberra 1988, p.263.

46
George Augustus Robinson, Journal 25 January 1838, in N.J.B. Plomley, *Weep in Silence. A History of the Flinders Island Aboriginal Settlement*, Blubber Head Press, Hobart 1987, p.525.

47
Rebe Taylor, op. cit., p.22.

48
See image of painting online at http://shapingtasmania.tmag.tas.gov.au/object.aspx?ID=84

49
Rebe Taylor, in 'The National Confessional', op. cit. (p.22), states, "Clive Turnbull, author of the strident 1948 book *Black War*, assumes Truganini is the woman standing next to Robinson, the woman who tried to save her people from extinction. Vivienne Rae-Ellis, in her controversial 1976 book *Trucanini: Queen or Traitor?* asserts Truganini is the woman pulling Woureddy to meet Robinson: the traitor who helped lead her people to extinction. But Tim Bonyhady and N.J.B. Plomley have since identified Truganini as the woman in the far right corner of the painting, ('almost out of sight') as Lyndall Ryan puts it."

50
Stephen Scheding, op. cit., p.119.

51
David Hansen, op. cit., p.48.

52
Lyndall Ryan, op. cit., p.155.

53
Hobart Town Courier, 20 December 1833, p.2.

54
Trumpeter General, 31 December 1833, p.2.

55
N.J.B. Plomley, 'Thomas Bock's portraits of the Tasmanian Aborigines', 1991, op. cit., p.37.

56
David Hansen, op. cit., p.52.

Gaye Sculthorpe acknowledges the generous help and advice of Sandra Bowdler, David Hansen, Mary McMahon and Jane Stewart.

Biographies of portrayed Aboriginal people

The names of Aboriginal people listed below are given in *palawa kani*, the reconstructed Aboriginal language of Tasmania.

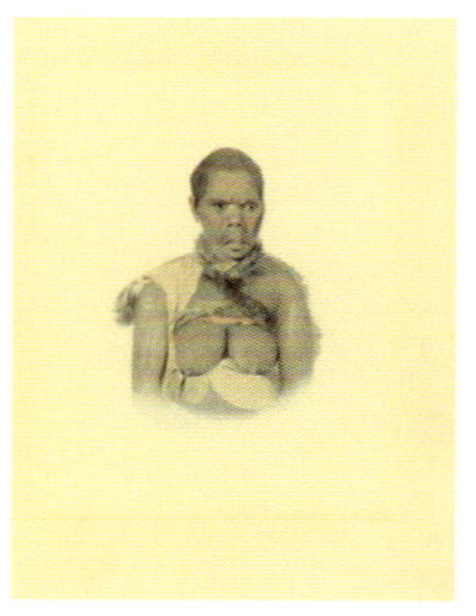

Laratung (c. 1792–1837) from the region of Robbins Island in northwest Tasmania. After being captured in July 1832, she was exiled to Flinders Island about 3 November 1832. She revisited Hobart briefly in December 1832, returning to Flinders Island where she died after a long illness in 1837. It was likely that her portrait was painted during her visit to Hobart.

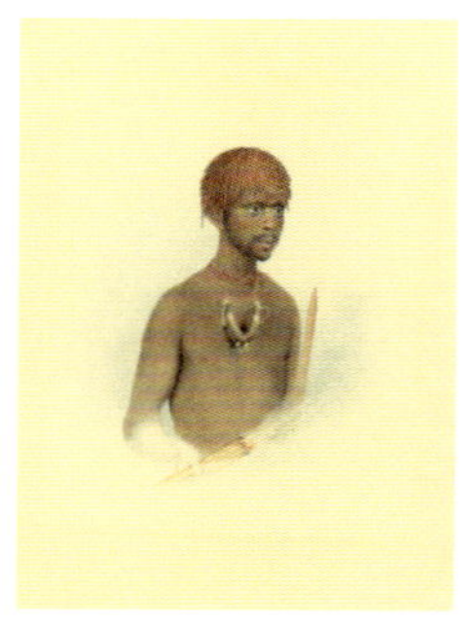

Malapuwinarana (c. 1812–42) was from the Cape Portland region of the North East Nation. He travelled with George Augustus Robinson across Tasmania from 1830 until 1835 when he was exiled to Flinders Island. With others, he was taken by Robinson to Melbourne in 1839. After being convicted of killing two whalers, he was hanged before a crowd of 5,000 people in 1842 in Melbourne's first execution.

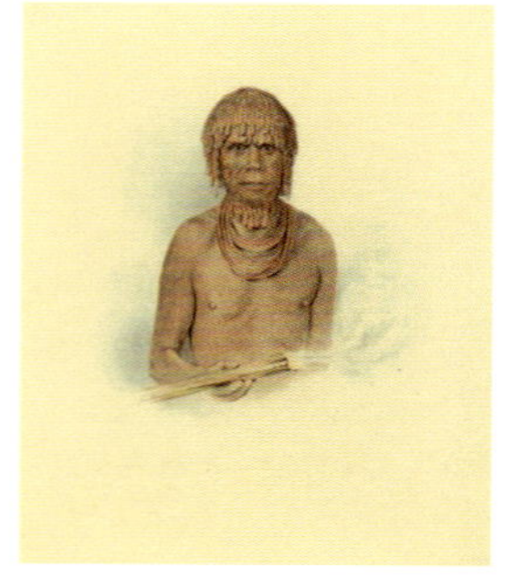

Manalakina (c. 1770–1835) was a powerful and revered leader of the Pairrebeenne clan of the North East Nation near Cape Portland. His second wife was Tanalipunya. After fiercely defending his country against British colonists, he joined the group travelling with George Augustus Robinson in search of other Aboriginal people. Despite earlier promises to the contrary, he was sent, to Flinders Island in September 1835. He died there in exile a few months later, not long after the death of his wife. He had a large family and there are many descendants alive today.

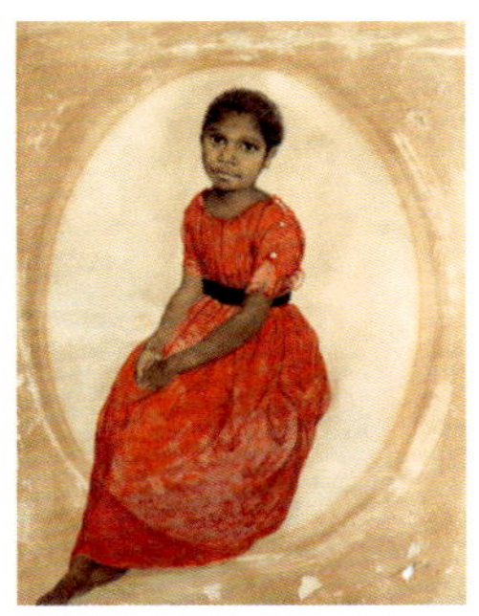

Mithina (1835–52) was born at Wybalena, the Aboriginal settlement at Flinders Island. Her parents, Tawtara and Wunganip, were from the South West Nation and had been exiled to Flinders Island in 1833. After the death of her parents, she was "adopted" by Sir John and Lady Franklin in 1839 and lived at Government House in Hobart for five years. When they returned to England in 1843, Mithina spent time at the Queens Orphan School, Flinders Island, and from1851 was living at Oyster Cove. After life at Government House, she found her changed circumstances challenging. She drowned c. 1852, after heavy drinking. Lady Franklin commissioned her portrait.

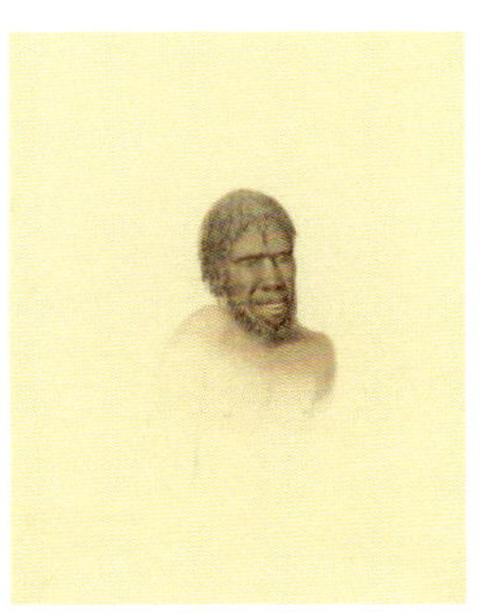

Multiyalakina (c. 1798–1832) was a leader of the Stoney Creek people of central Tasmania and a great song man and story teller. Between 1826 and 1828 he led raids against the British colonists stealing his lands. He was captured in late 1828 and spent a year in Richmond prison. Skilfully engaging with Europeans and his own kin, he travelled with protector George Augustus Robinson in south west Tasmania in 1830. For a short time, he joined the "Black Line" seeking to corral Aborigines still at large on the island. He joined Robinson's group again in search of the Big River people in late 1831. He died in hospital in Launceston and was buried there in 1832.

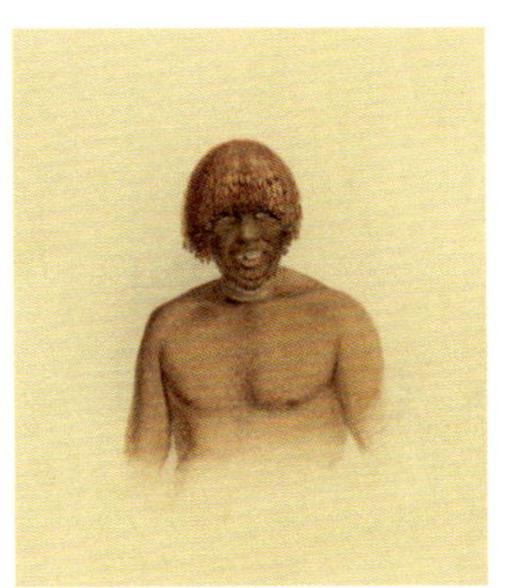

Muntipiliyata (?–c. 1836) was the celebrated leader of the Big River people. He evaded capture or killing by colonists but eventually surrendered in December 1831. With a large group of his kinsfolk, he was paraded before Lieutenant-Governor Arthur and residents of Hobart in January 1832. He was exiled to Flinders Island where he died before 1836. His portrait was likely made in Hobart after his capture.

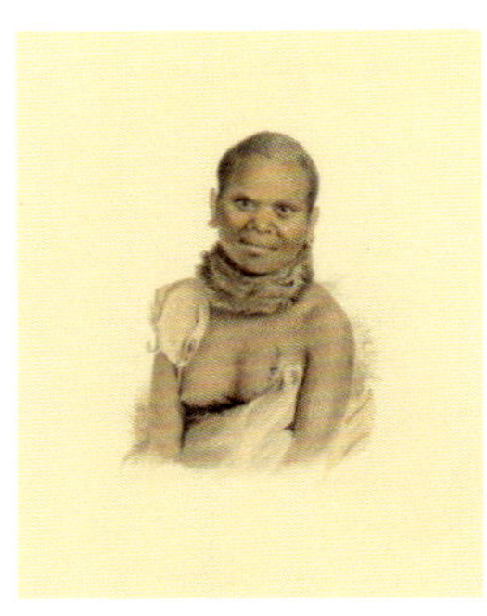

Namplut (c. 1815–39) was from the Great Lakes region in central Tasmania and was the partner of Malapuwinarana. She accompanied George Augustus Robinson for many years in his travels across Tasmania. She was exiled to Flinders Island in September 1835 where she died.

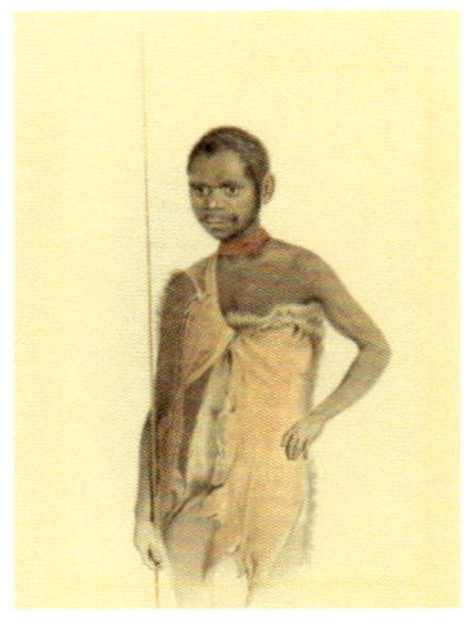

Prupilathina (c. 1817–41) was from central Tasmania, north of Great Lake. He travelled with George Augustus Robinson from August 1831 to 1835. When exiled to Flinders Island, he continued traditional practices such as wearing of ochre and performing ceremony. With others, he went with Robinson to Port Phillip in 1839, where he drowned at Westernport in January 1841. Also an artist, his painting of a native hen, dated 1835, is one of the earliest surviving drawings by a Tasmanian Aborigine.

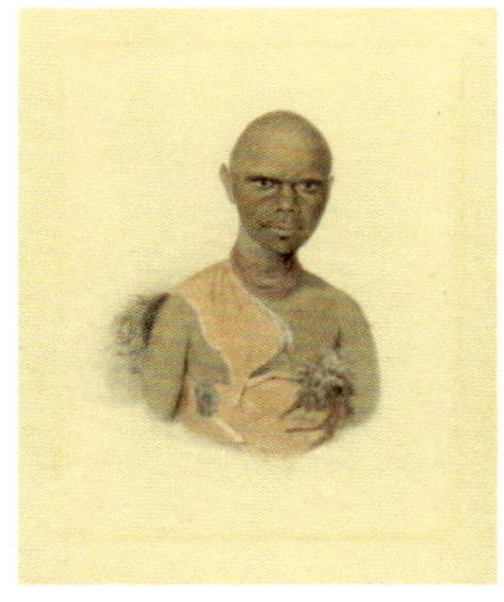

Tanalipunya (c. 1806–35) was from the region of Little Swanport, part of the North East Nation. She was abducted by sealer John Brown. Like many Aboriginal women at that time living with sealers, she was subjected to flogging and mistreatment. She became the wife of Manalakina and travelled for four years with George Augustus Robinson from October 1830. She died in Hobart in May 1835.

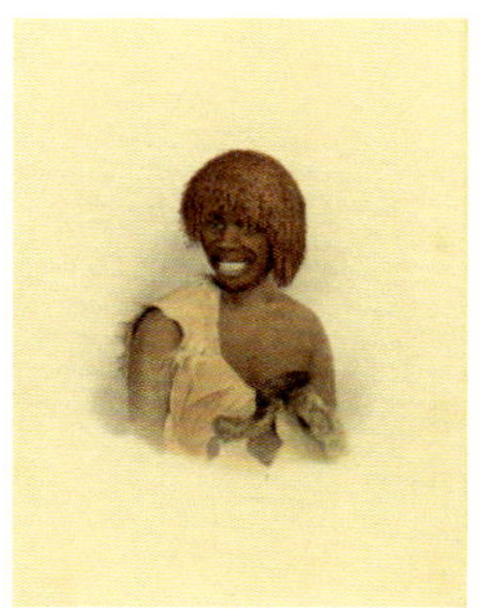

Tanaminawayt (c. 1812–42) was from the region of Cape Grim in northwest Tasmania. After his people were decimated, he travelled with George Augustus Robinson from June 1830. With others, he was taken by Robinson to Melbourne in 1839. After he and Malapuwinarana were convicted of killing two whalers, he was hanged before a crowd of 5,000 people in 1842 in Melbourne's first execution.

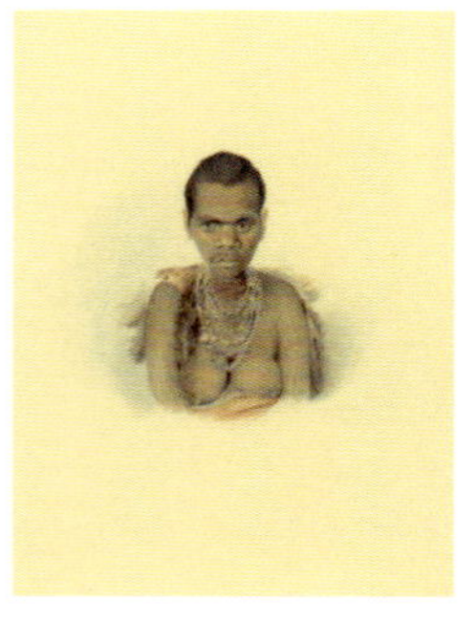

Trukanini (c. 1812–76) was from the South East Nation near Recherche Bay. She was the second wife of Wurati. Famously but erroneously believed to be the last Tasmanian Aborigine when she died in 1876, she worked closely as a guide to Robinson for many years, and on one occasion, saved his life. After her death, her skeleton was dug up and put on display in the Tasmanian Museum and Art Gallery from 1905 to 1947 until it was returned to the Aboriginal community for a ceremonial farewell in 1976.

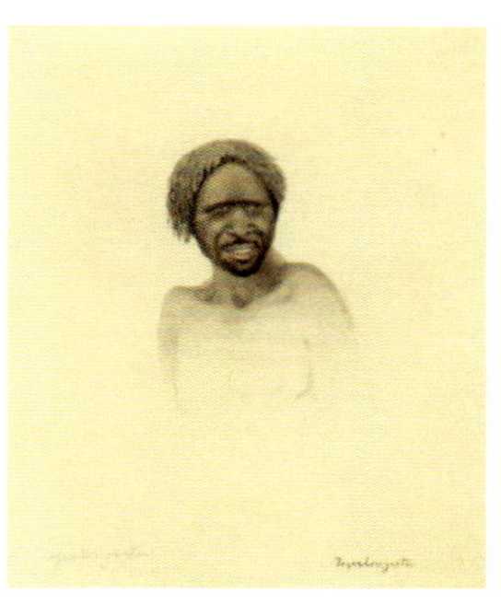

Tukalunginta (?–1837) was a leader of the Oyster Bay people. After evading capture or being killed by colonists for many months, he eventually surrendered with a large group of *palawa* in 1831. After being paraded with others before Lieutenant-Governor Arthur and residents of Hobart, he was exiled to Flinders Island in February 1832. He died there in 1837. His portrait was likely made in Hobart after his capture. Part of his arm and hand were amputated by trauma, possibly by a European man trap.

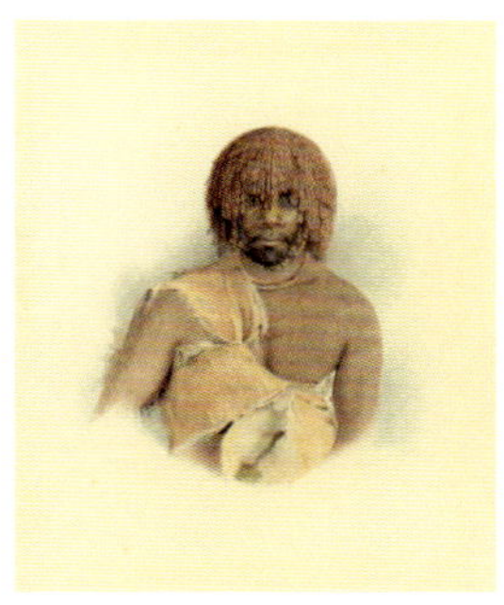

Wurati (c. 1784–1842) was from Bruny Island, part of the South East Nation and husband of Trukanini. His cultural knowledge was deep and respected. He travelled with George Augustus Robinson in Tasmania from 1829 and went with him to Port Phillip in 1839. He died just before arriving back at Flinders Island in 1842 and was buried on Big Green Island.

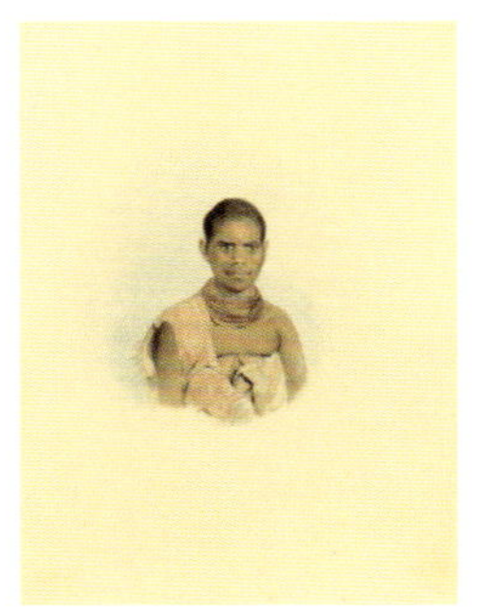

Wutapuwitja (c. 1807–45?) was from the George Town or Pipers River region, of the North East Nation. She was abducted by sealer Michael Mckenzie and later became the partner of Tanaminawayt. She travelled for some years with George Augustus Robinson in Tasmania, and also accompanied him, with others, to Port Phillip in 1839.

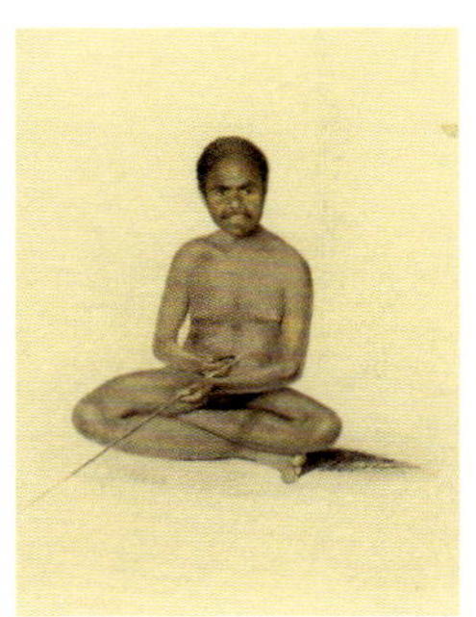

Youth sitting, 1831–35. This is possibly Joseph McLaine (c. 1806–?), a Hawaiian. After travelling from Hawaii to New York and then to England, he was convicted of a crime in Liverpool and sent as a convict to Tasmania in 1829. He worked as a convict servant to George Augustus Robinson during his travels with Aboriginal people around Tasmania c. 1830–32.

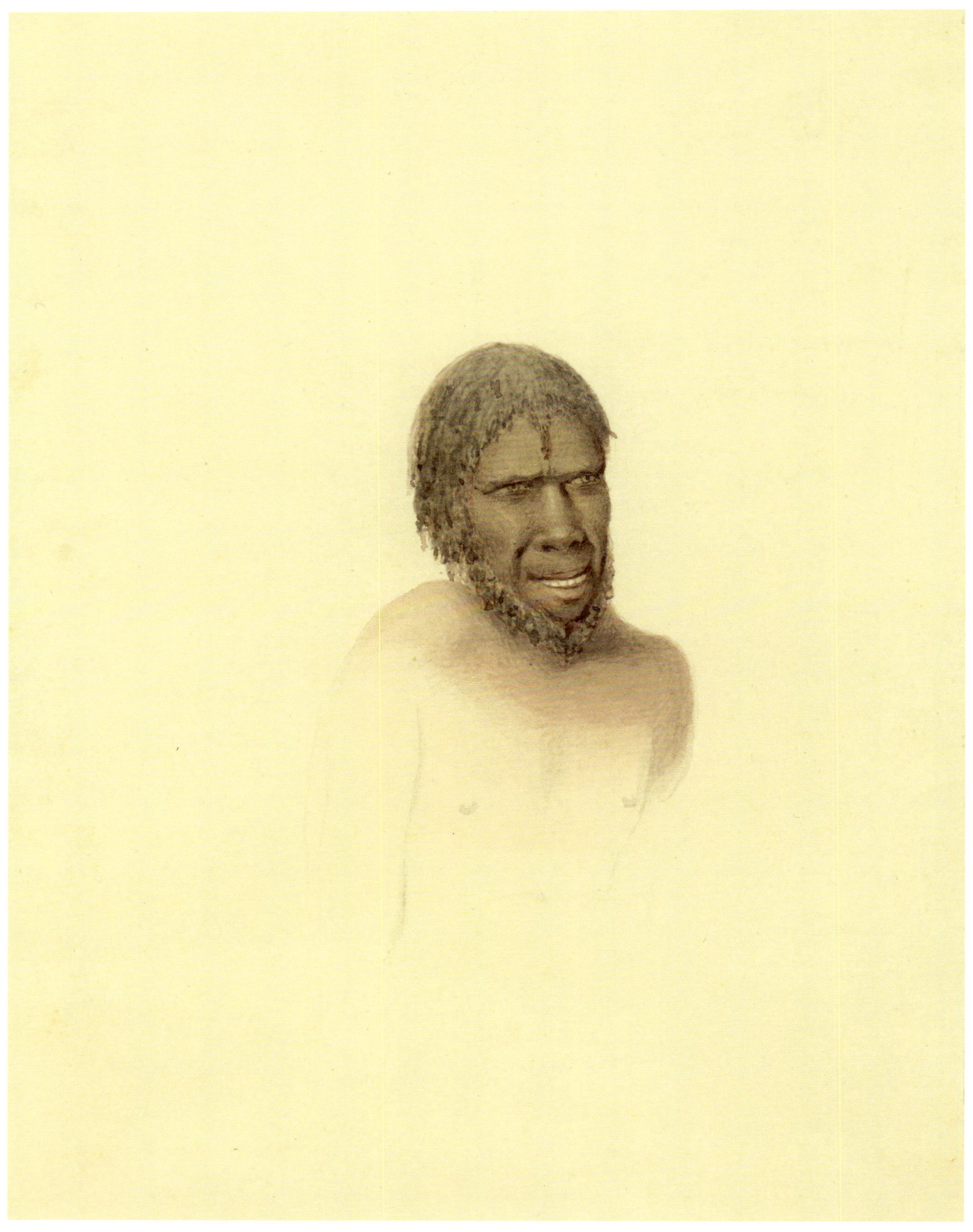

Untitled, probably **Multiyalakina** (Ehumarah, Umarrah), c. 1832

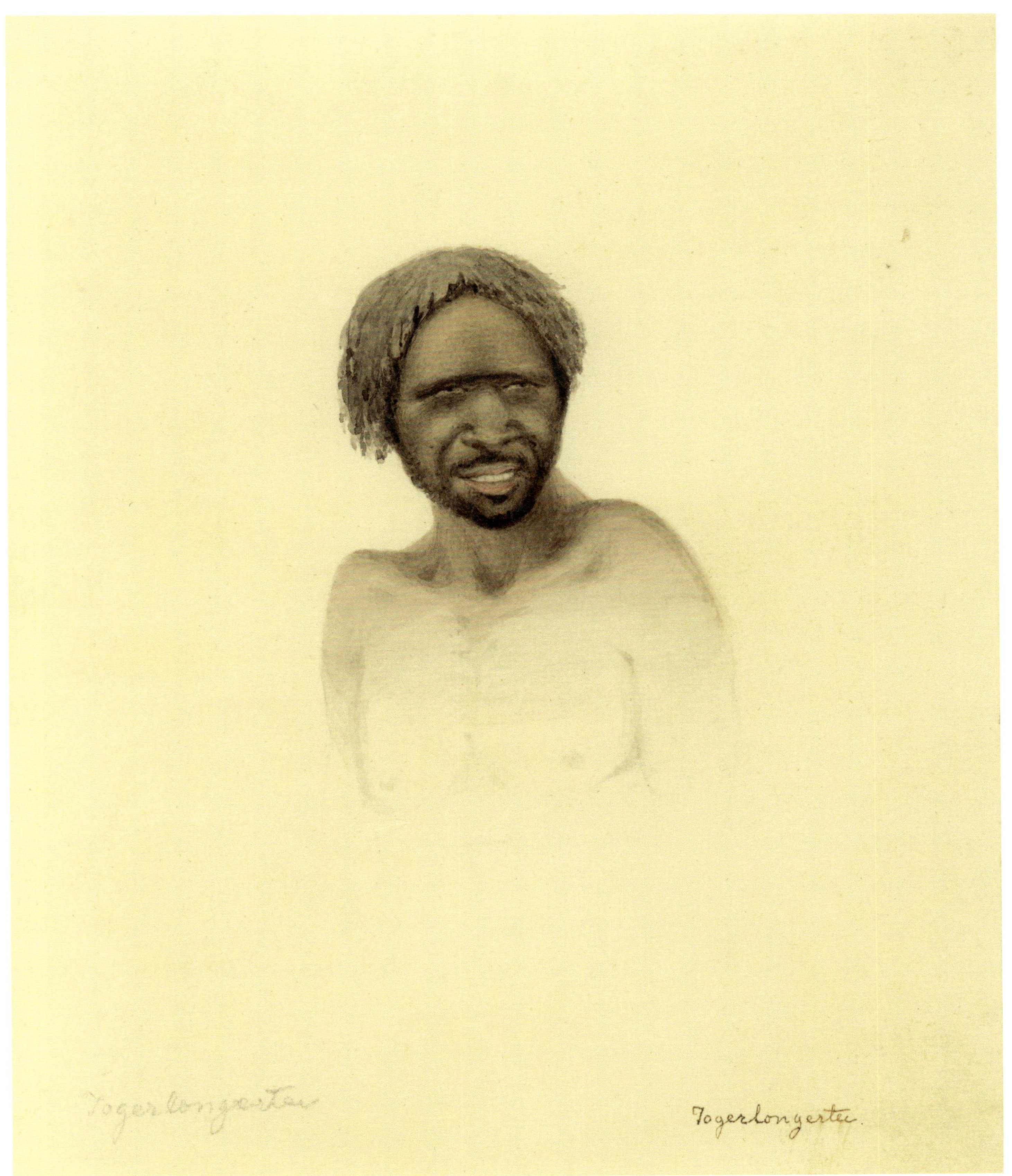

Tukalunginta (Togerlongerter), c. 1832–35

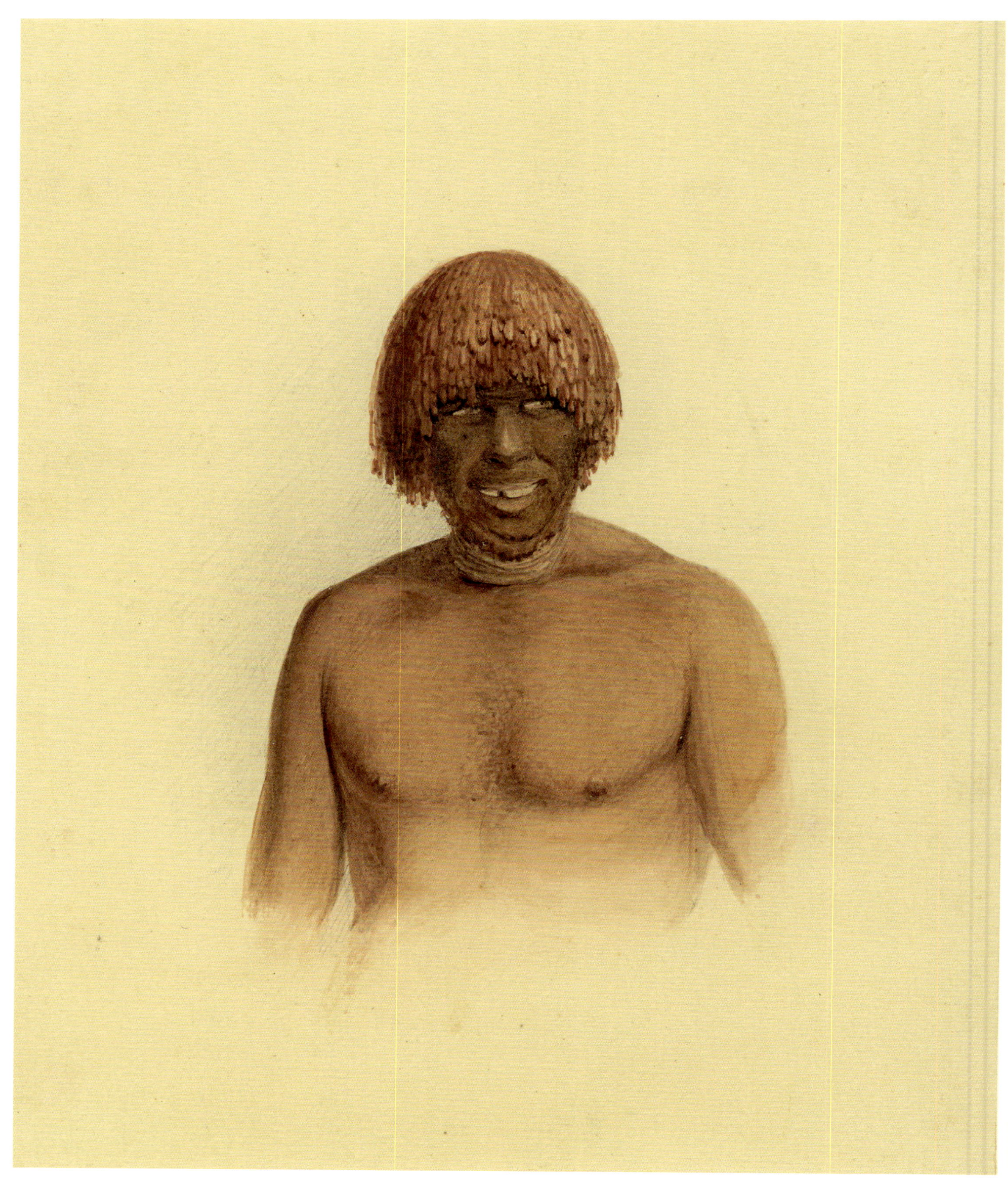

Untitled, probably **Muntipiliyata** (Montpelliater), c. 1832–35

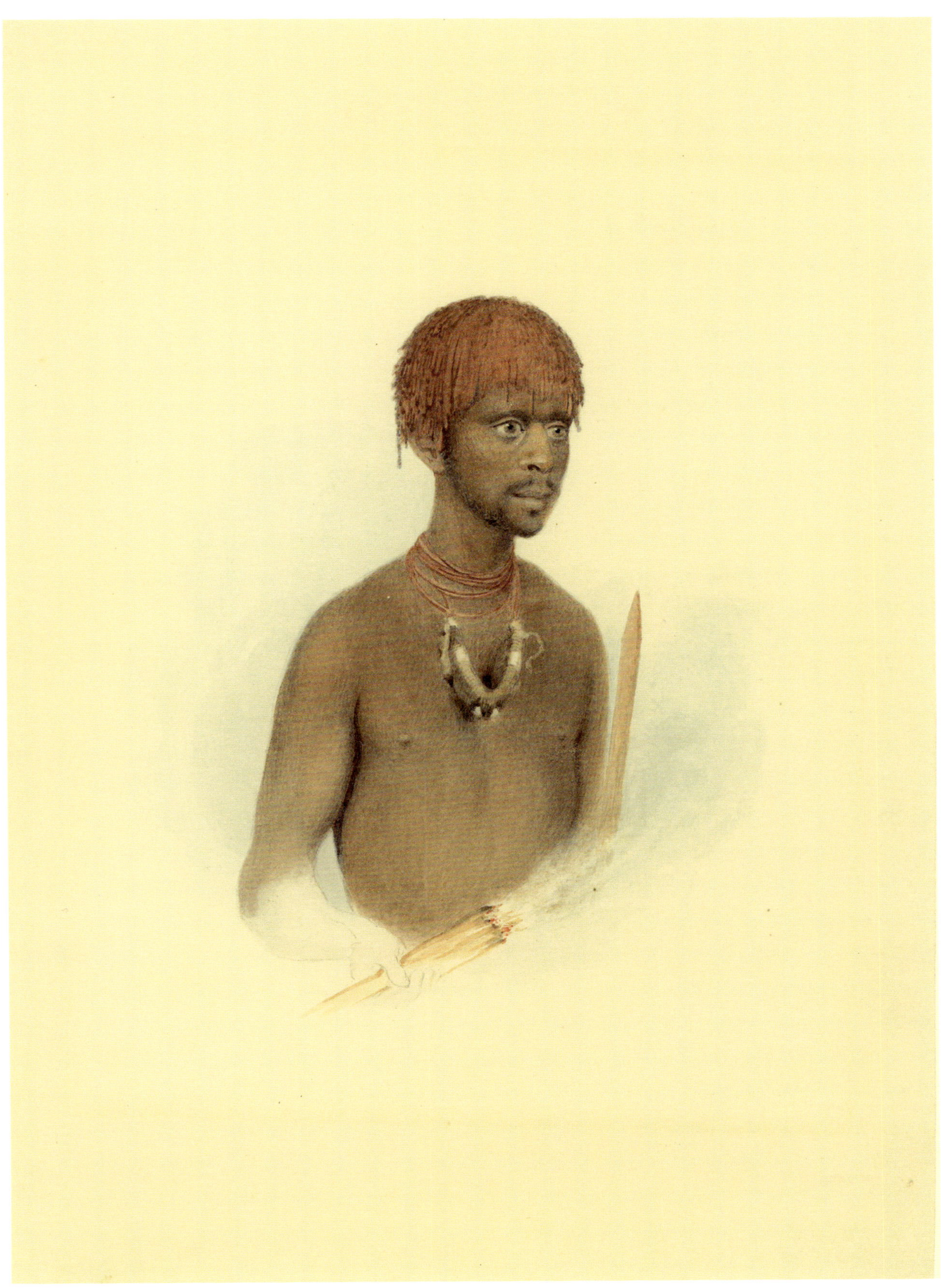

Untitled, **Malapuwinarana** (Maulboyheenner, Timmy), 1831–35

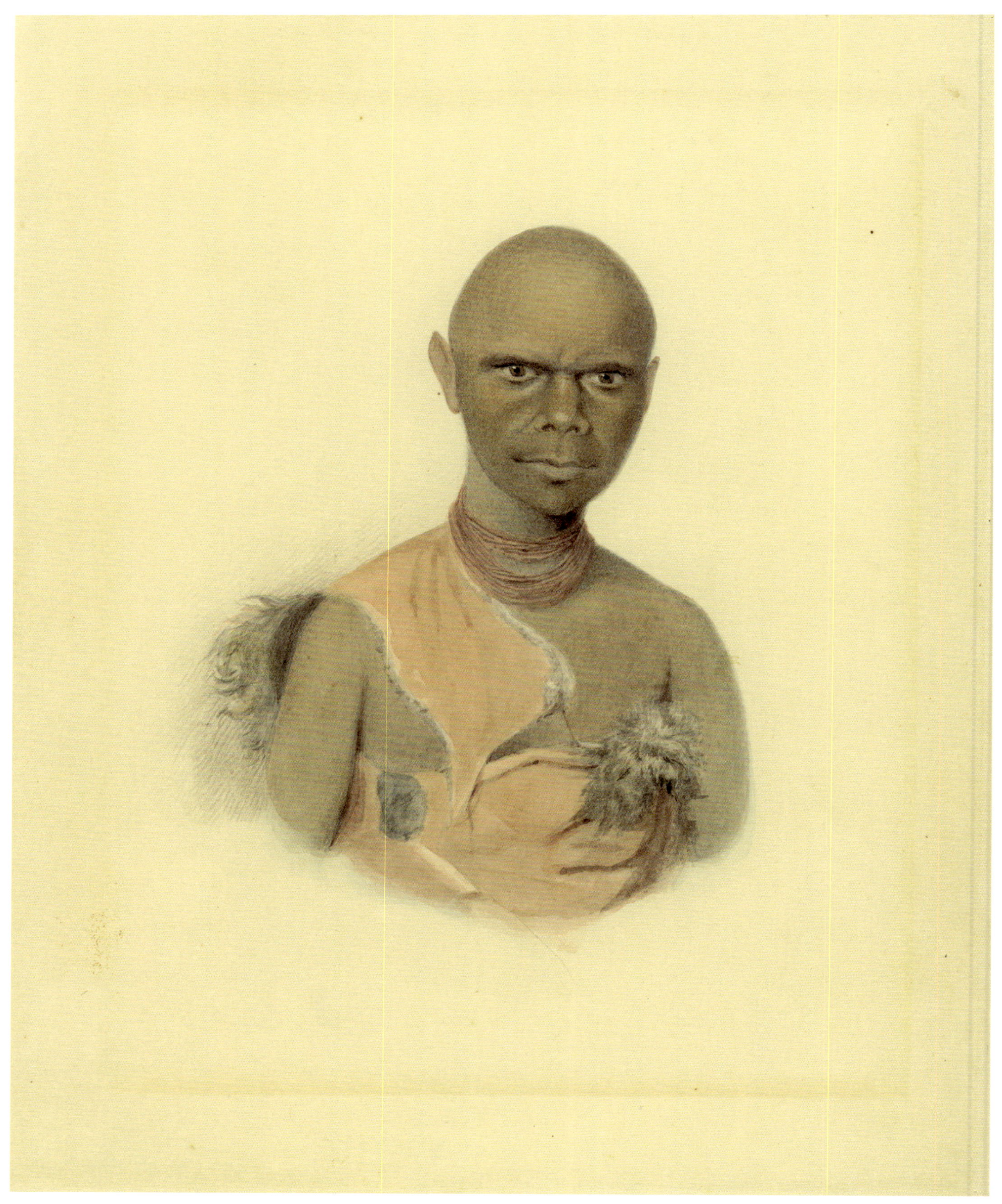

Untitled, probably **Tanalipunya** (Tanleboneyer, Sall), 1831–35

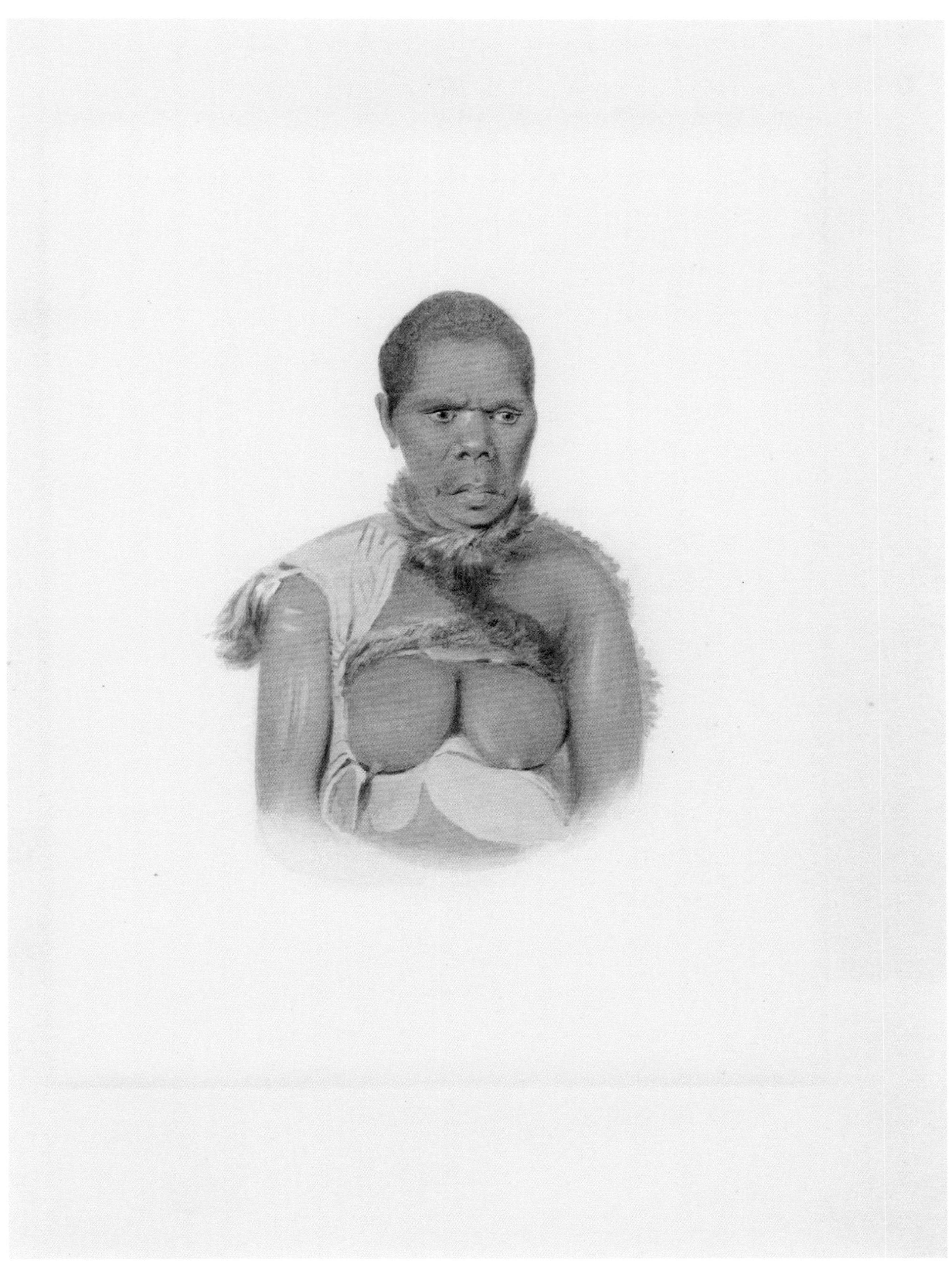

Untitled, **Laratung** (Larratong), 1832–35

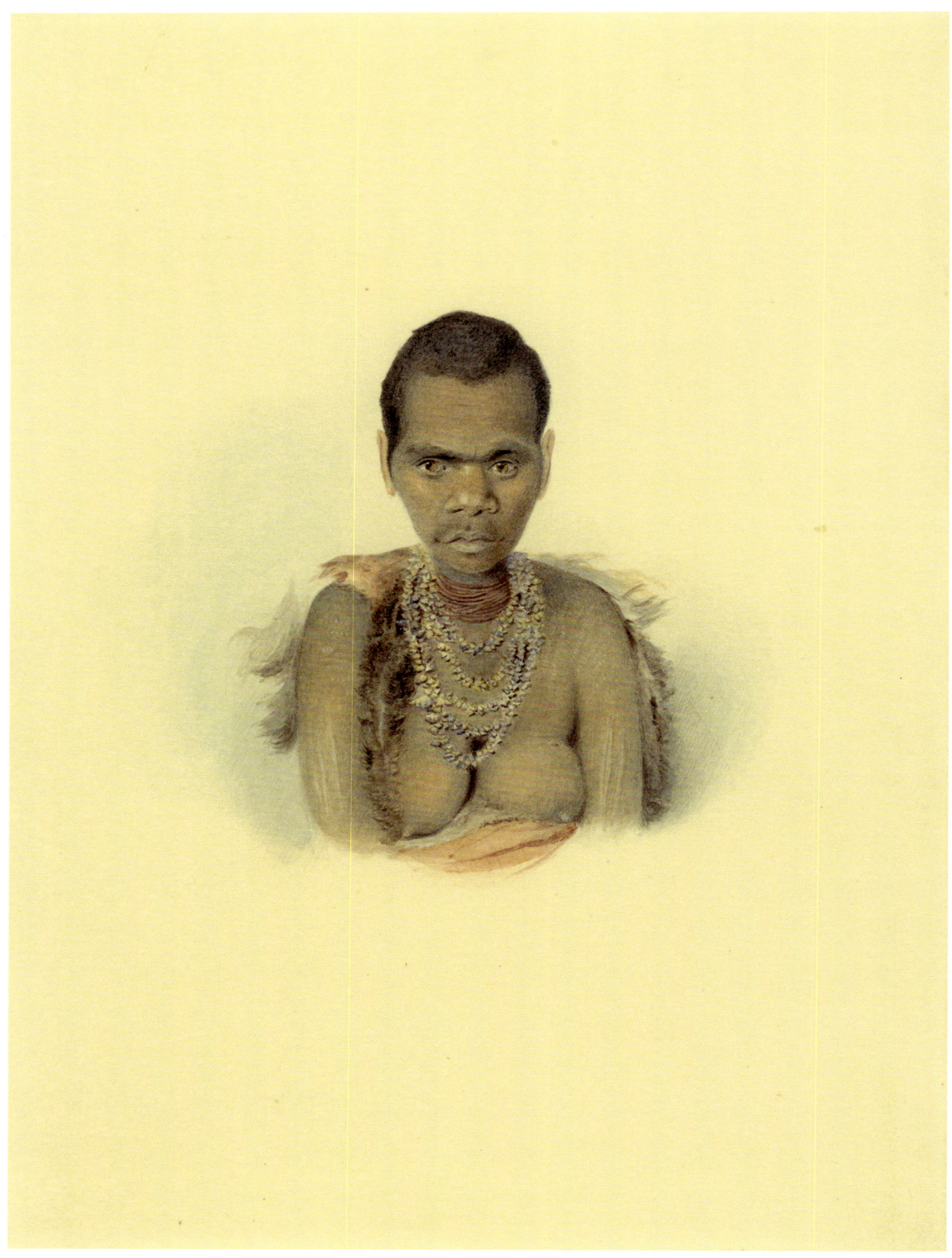

Untitled, **Trukanini** (Truganini, Truggernana), 1831

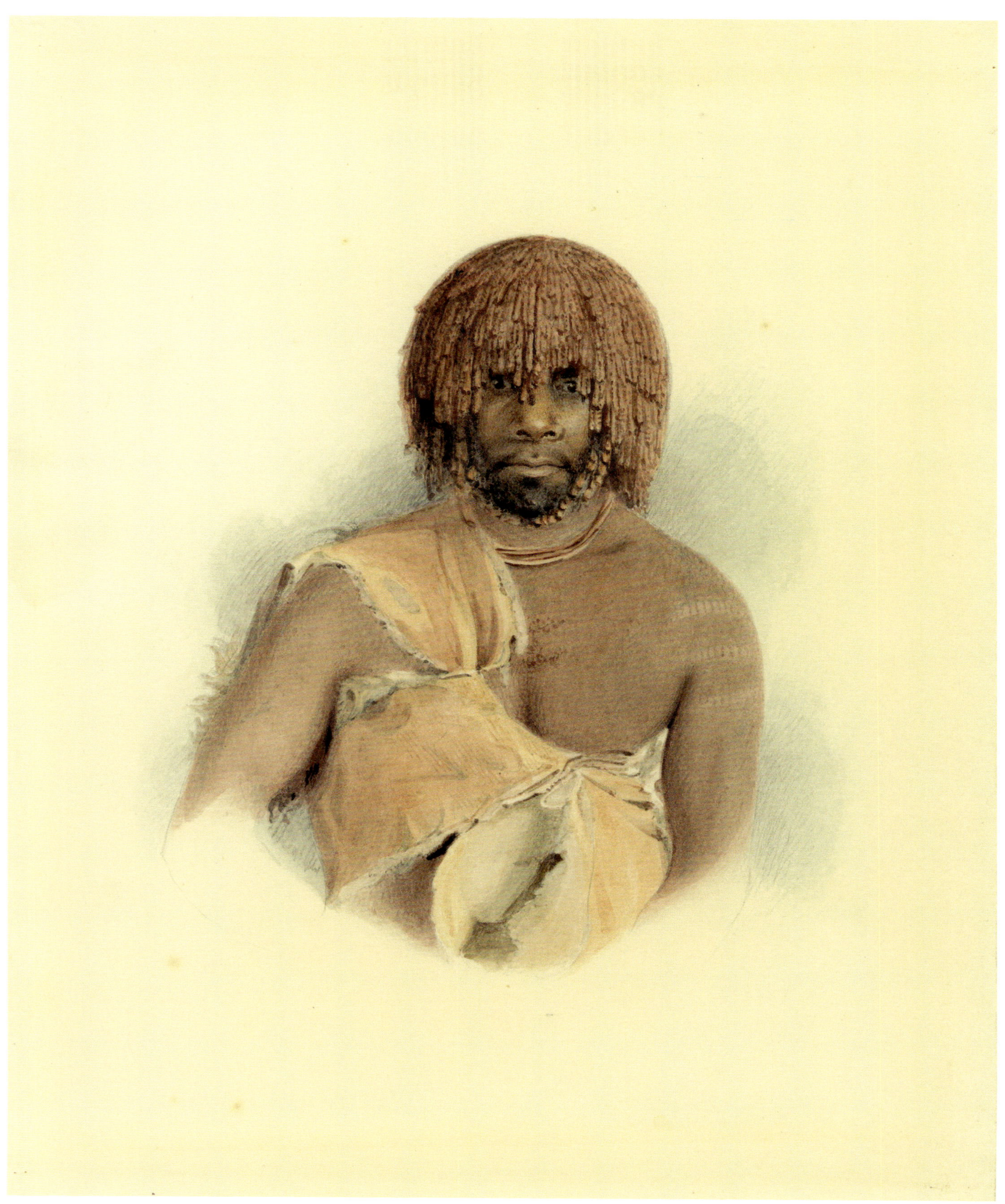

Untitled, **Wurati** (Woureddy), 1831

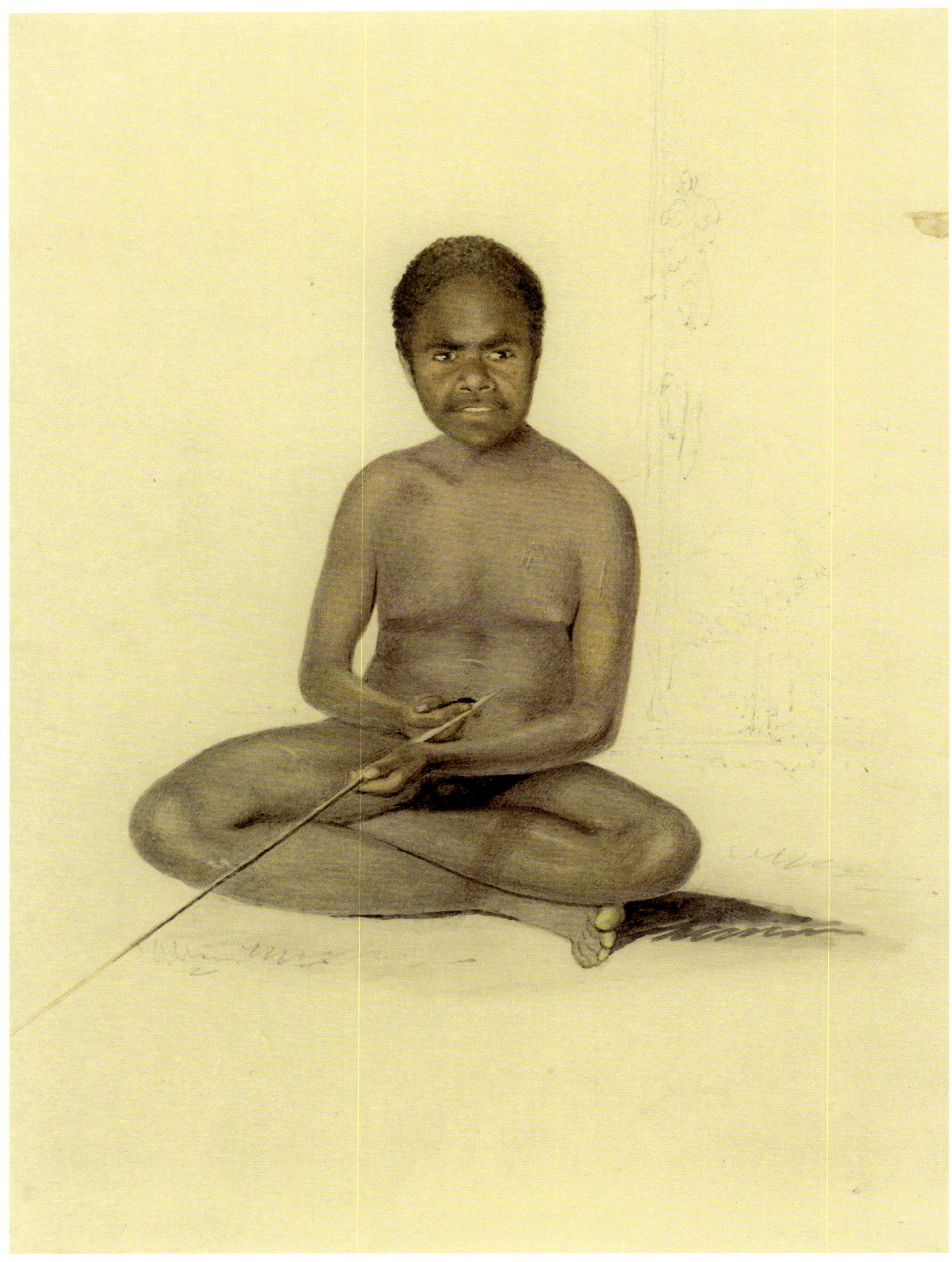

Untitled, **Youth sitting**, 1831–35

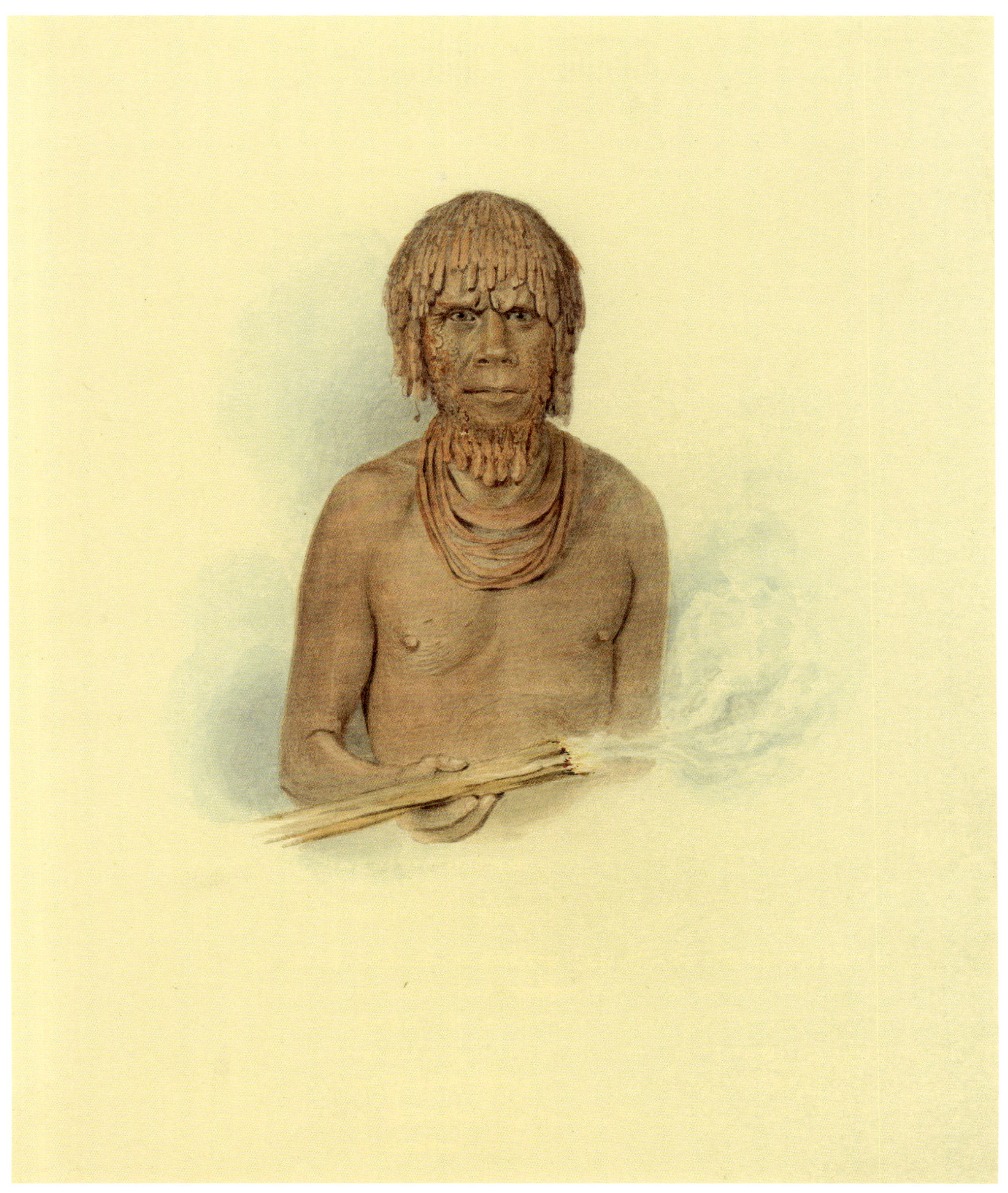

Untitled, **Manalakina** (Mannalargenna), 1831–35

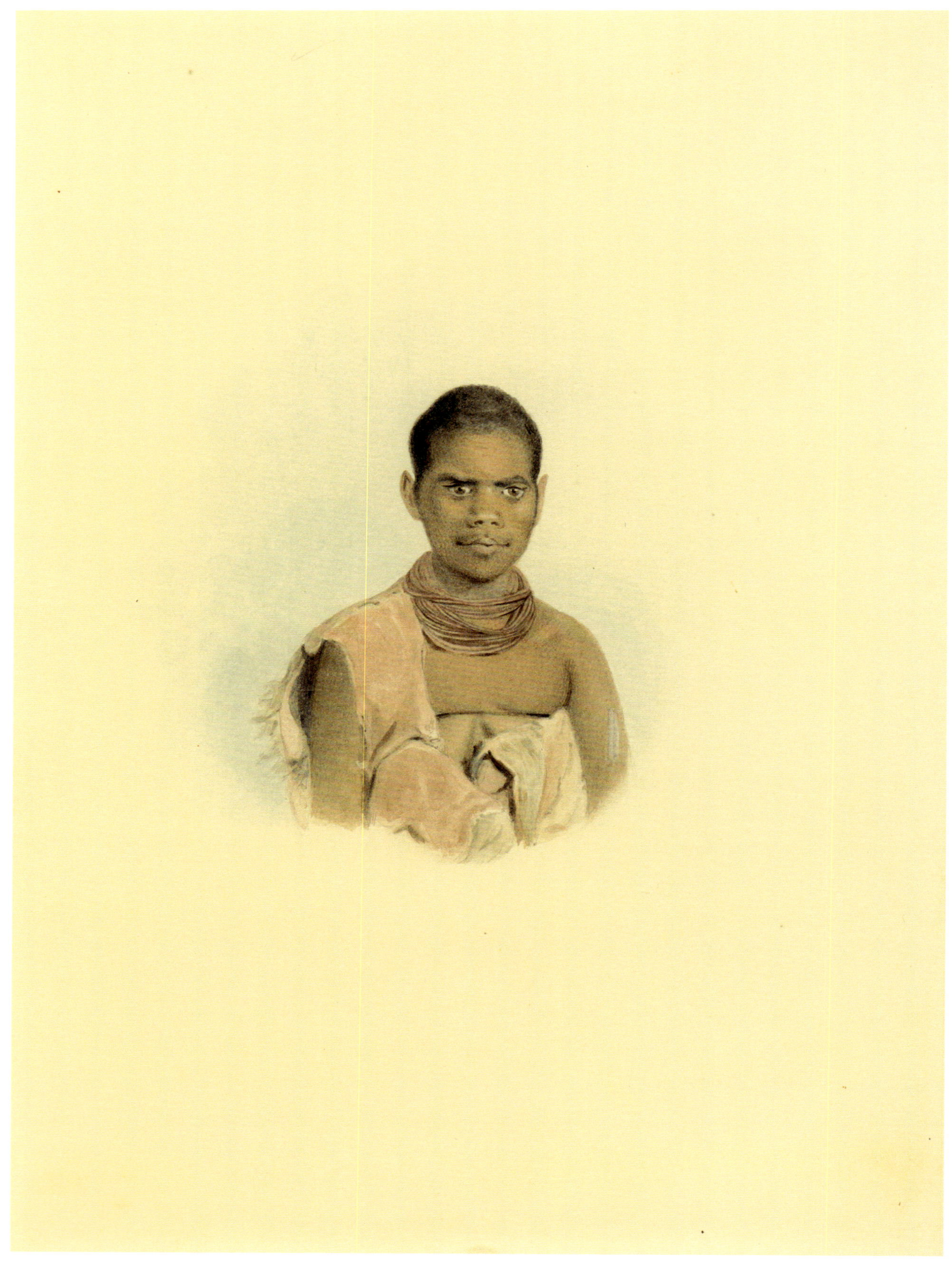

Untitled, **Wutapuwitja** (Wortabowigee, Fanny, Jock), 1832–35

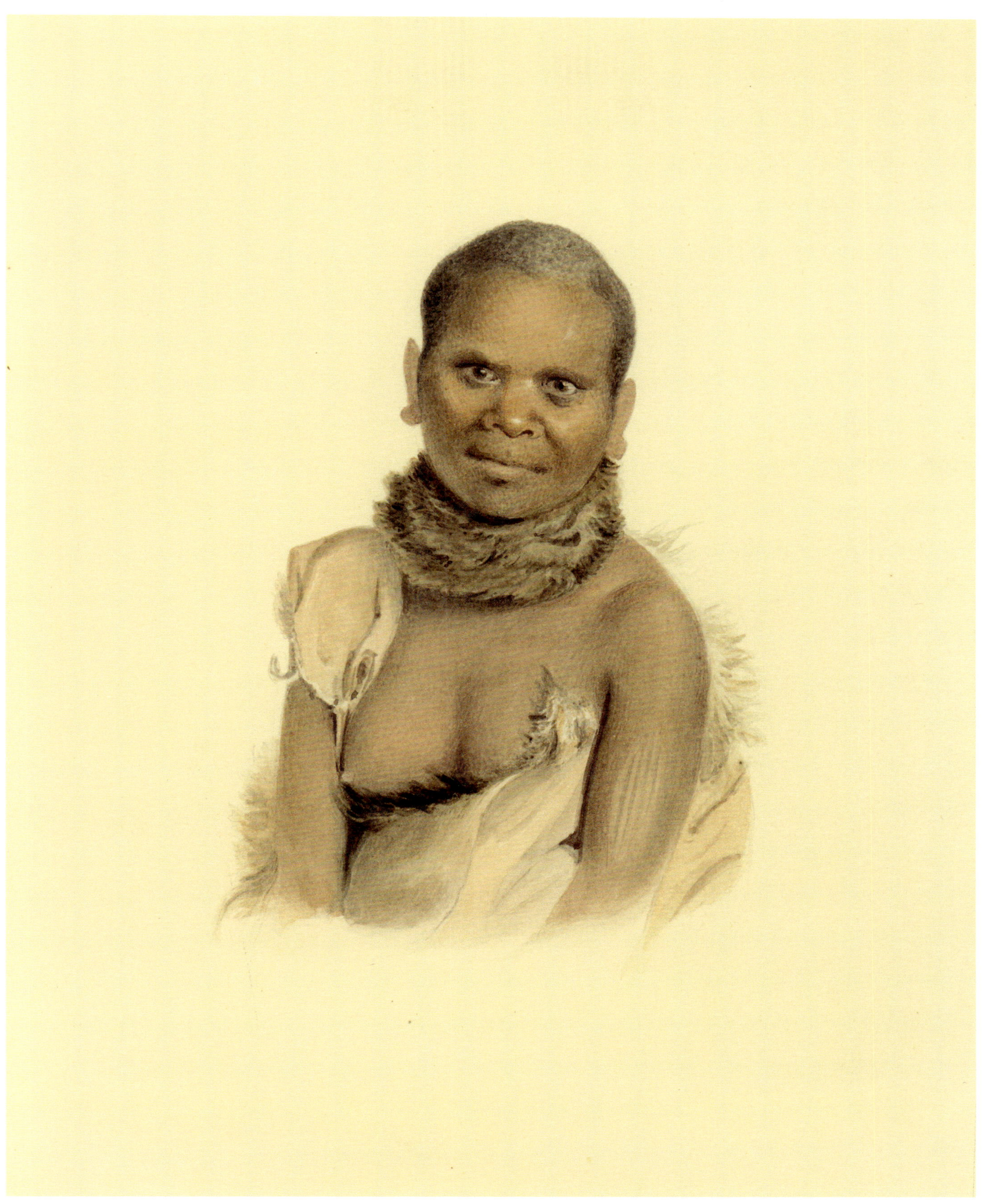

Untitled, **Namplut** (Numbloote, aka Jenny), 1831–35

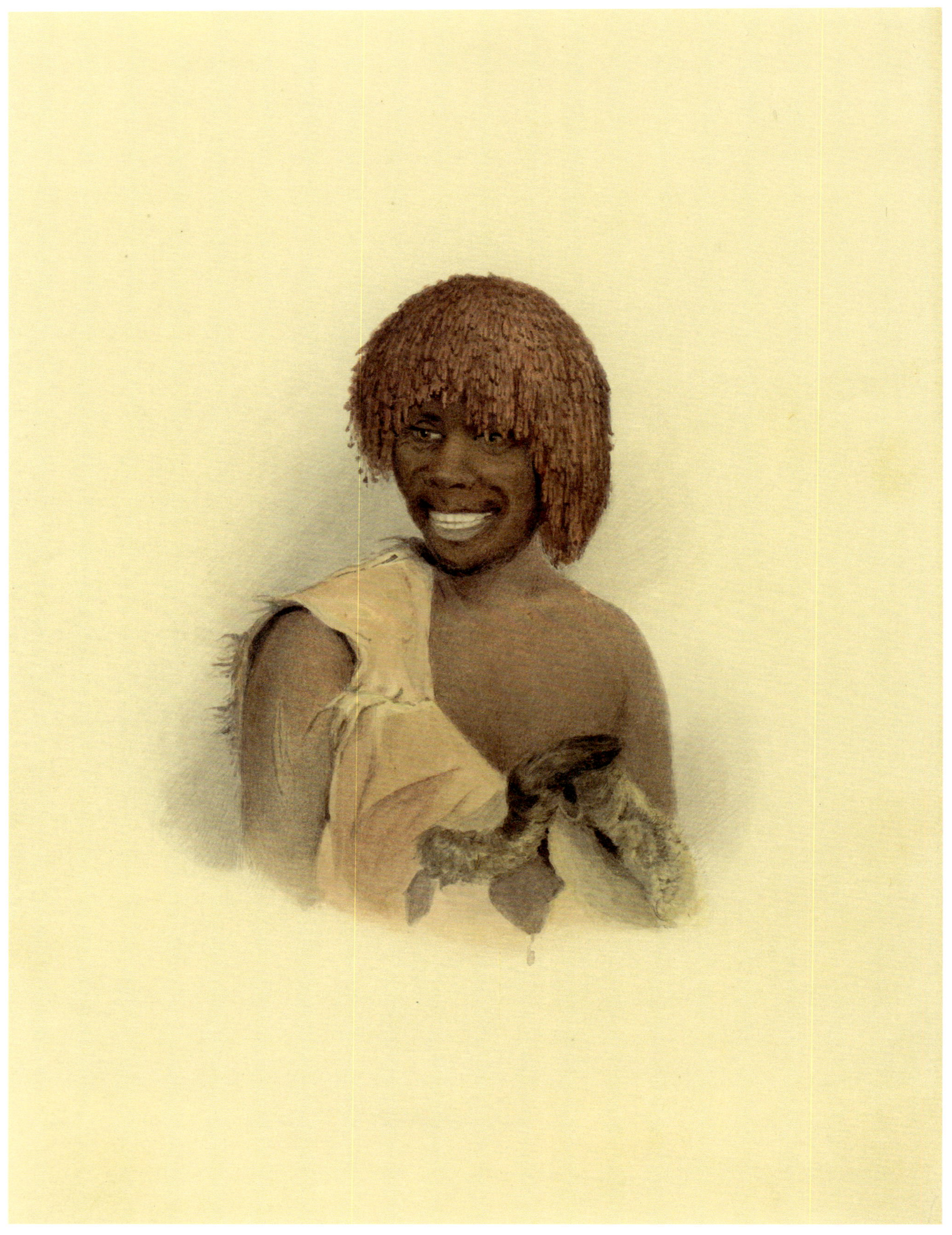

Untitled, **Tanaminawayt** (Tunnaminnerwate, Peevay, Jack), 1831–35

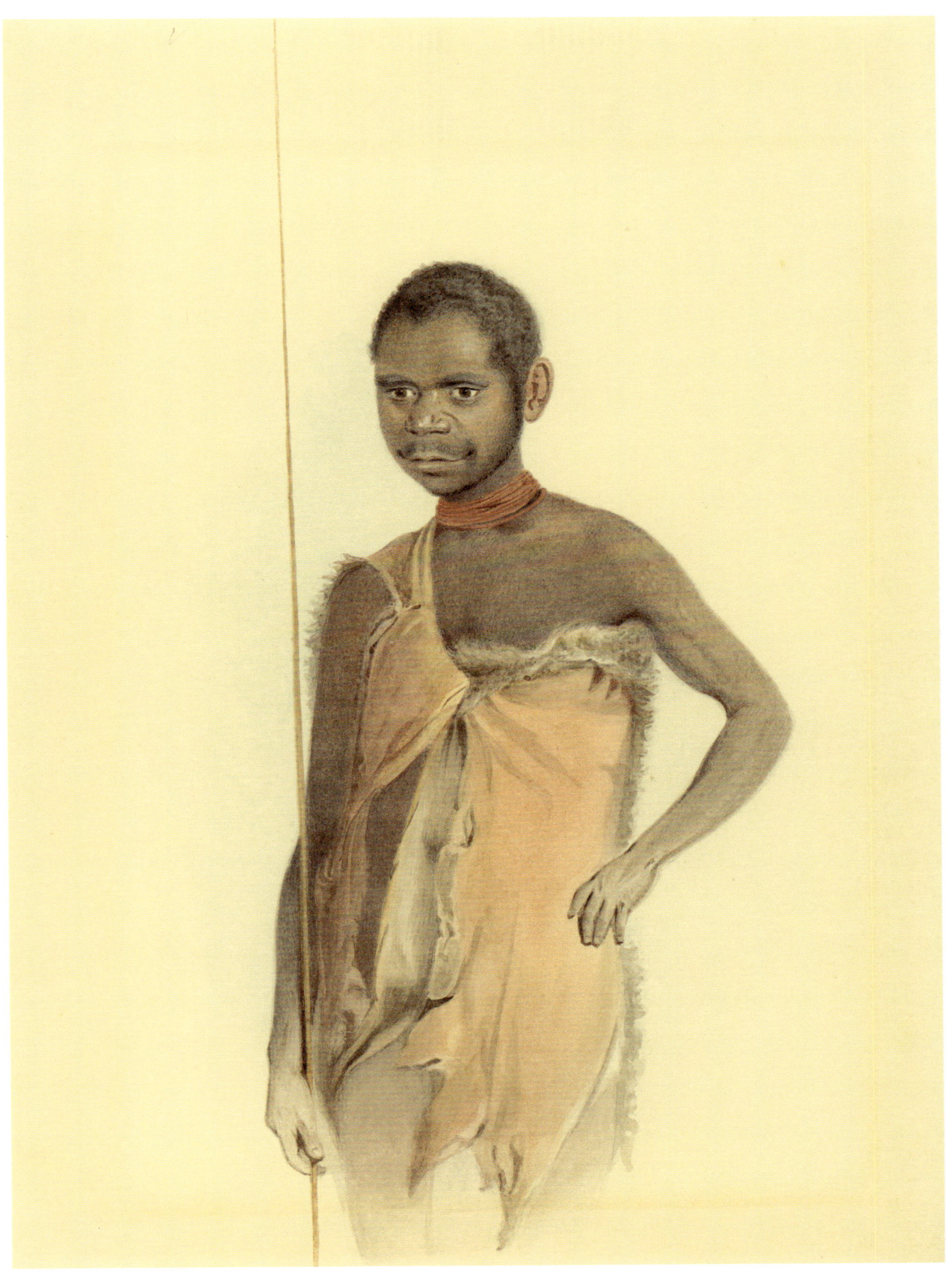

Untitled, **Prupilathina** (Probelatter, Lackerla, Jemmy, Jimmy), 1831–35

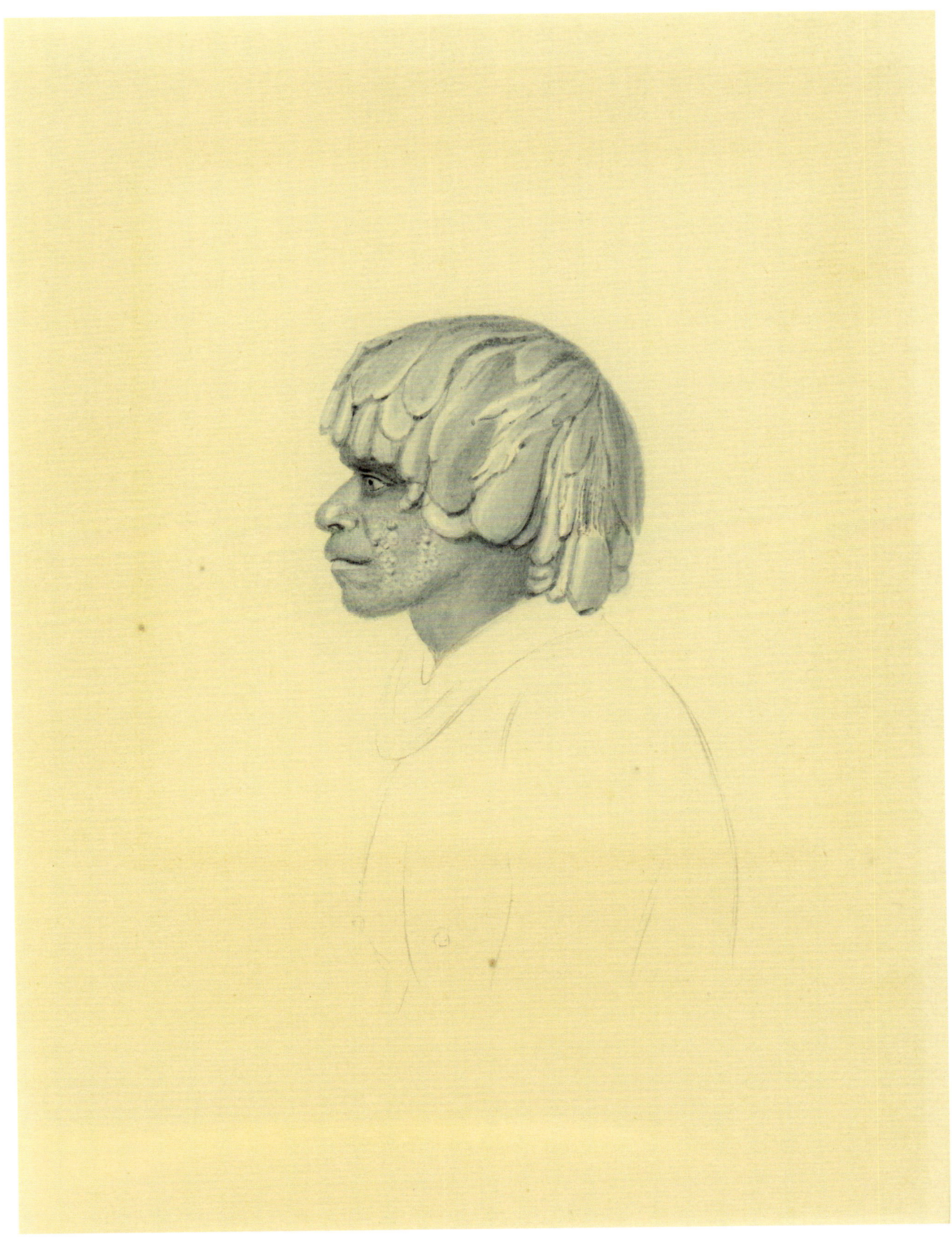

Untitled, **Manalakina** (Mannalargenna), 1831–35

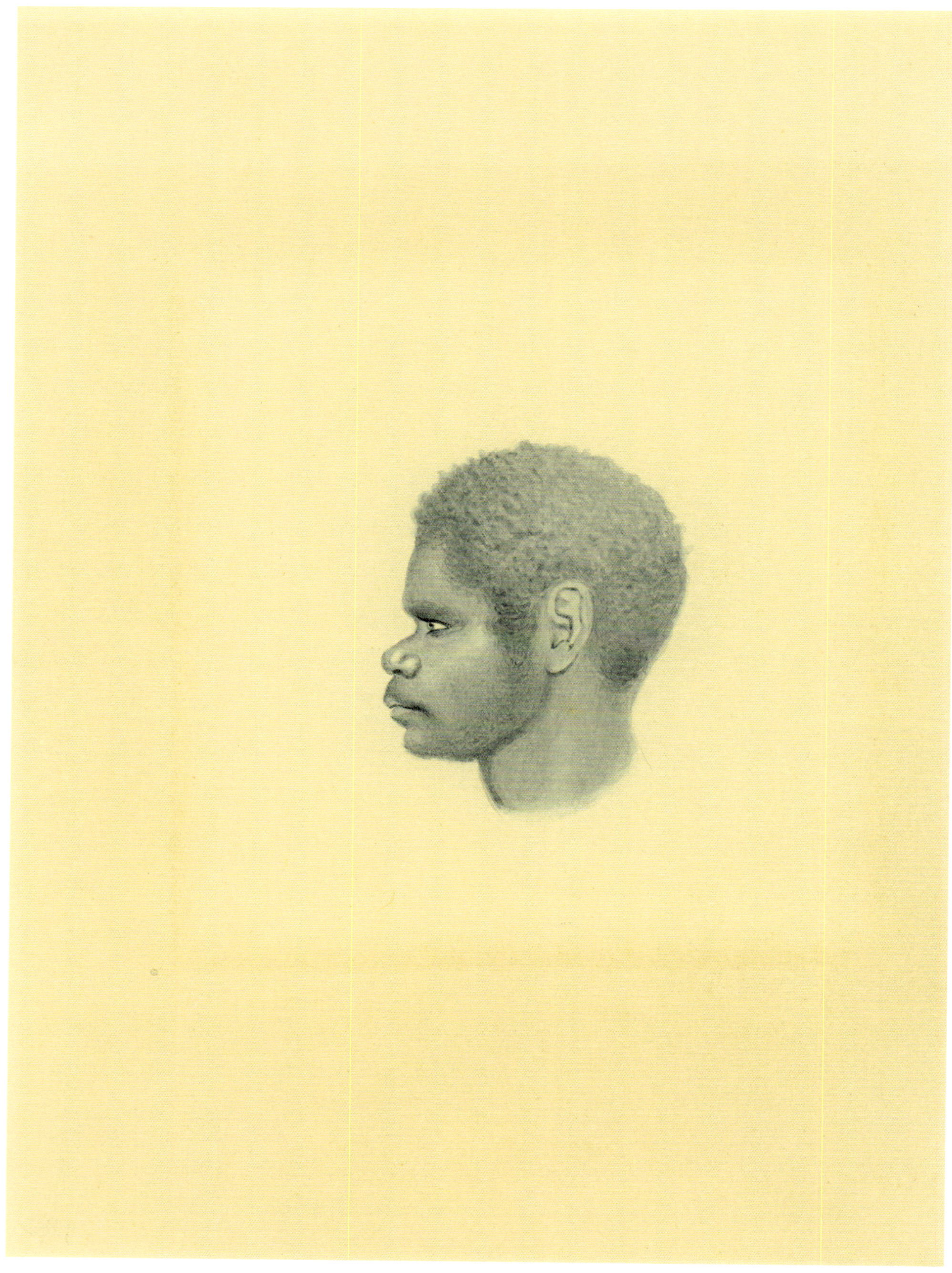

Untitled, **Prupilathina** (Probelatter, Lackerla, Jemmy, Jimmy), 1831–35

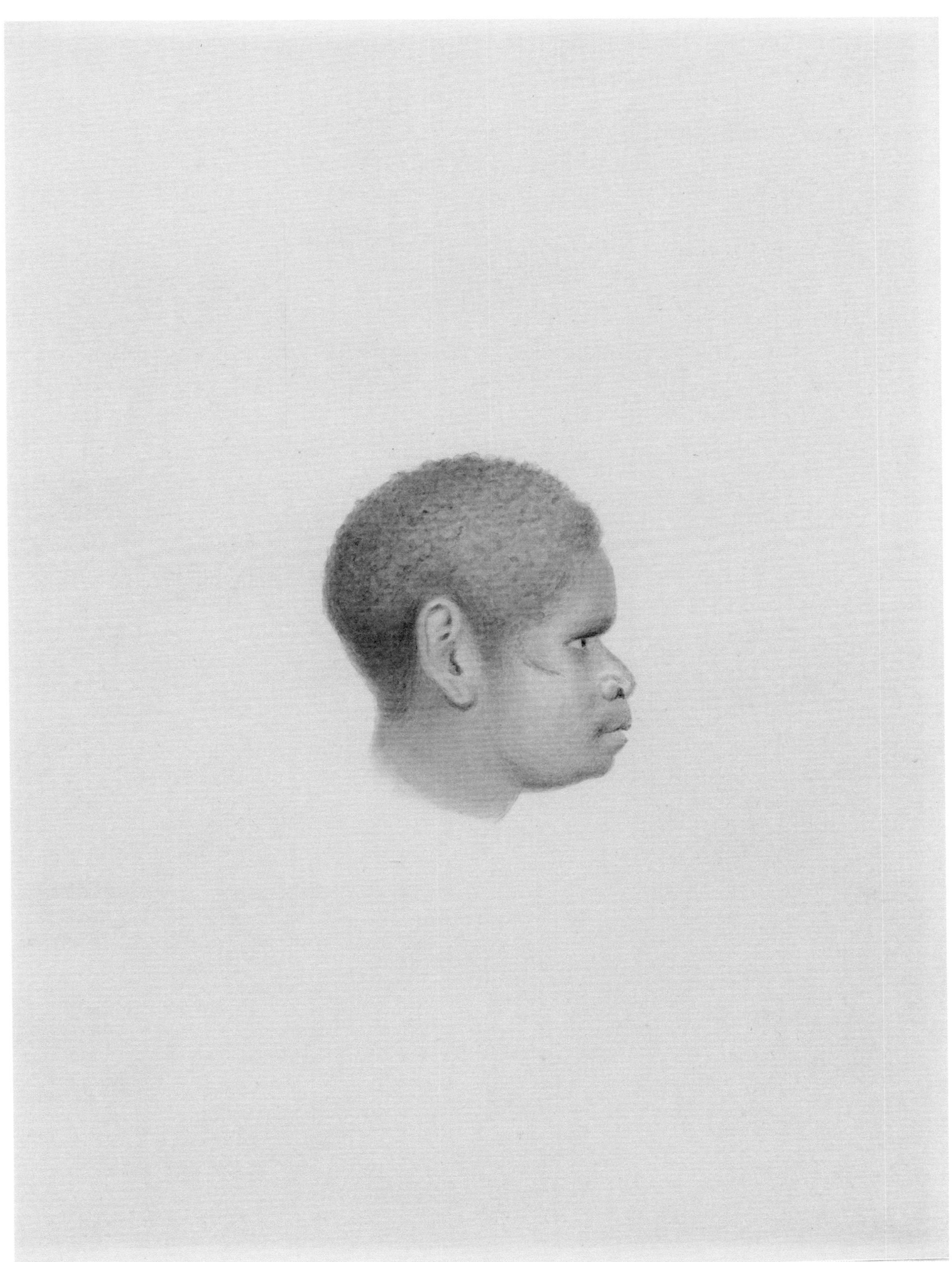

Untitled, **Namplut** (Numbloote, Jenny, Jinny), 1831–35

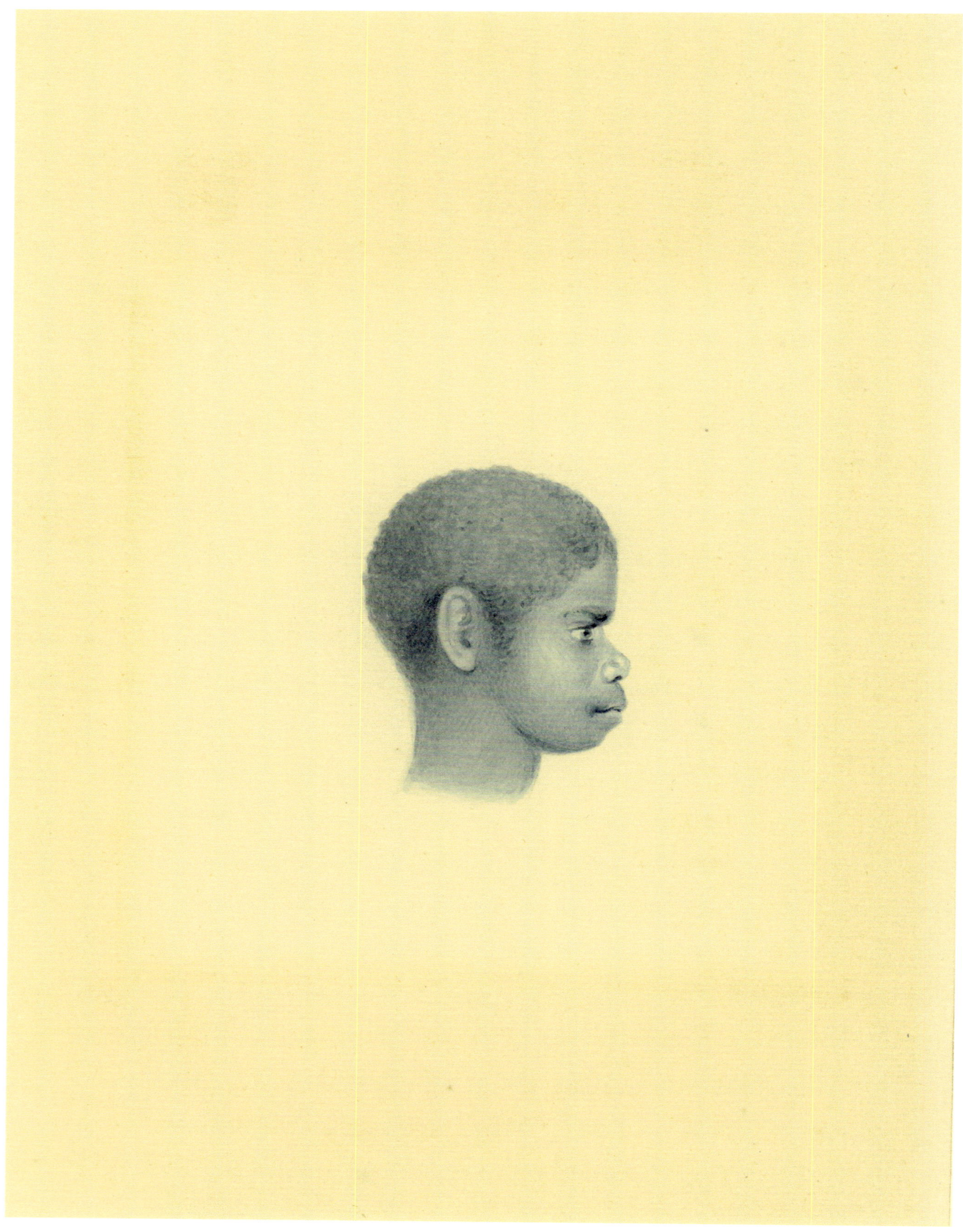

Untitled, **Trukanini** (Truganini, Truggernana), 1831–35

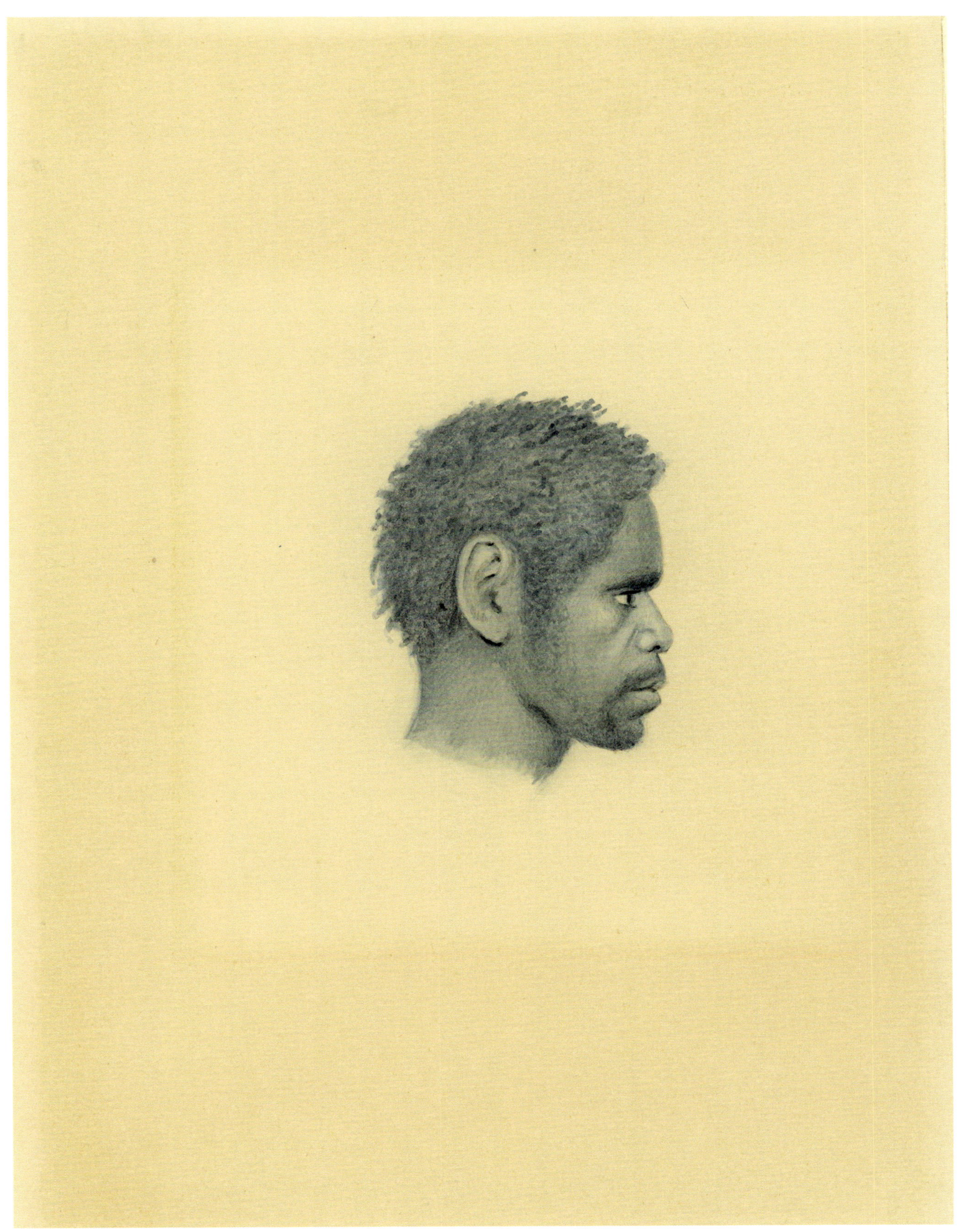

Untitled, **Malapuwinarana** (Maulboyheenner, Timmy), 1831–35

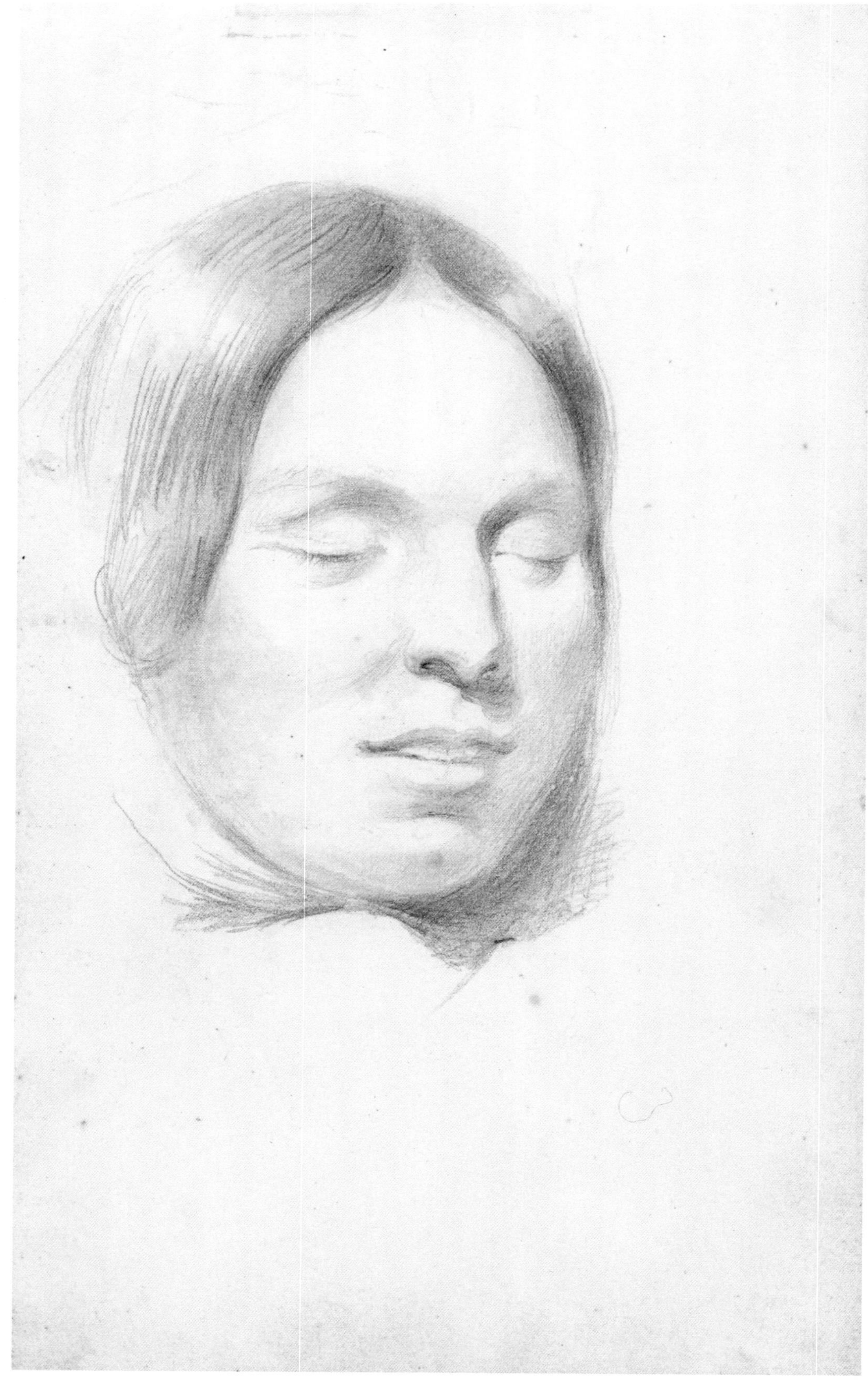

Page from **Sketchbook of post mortem studies**, c. 1835

Death and Thomas Bock

Hamish Maxwell-Stewart

One of the many unusual things about Thomas Bock is his penchant for drawing the dead. A remarkable series of post-mortem studies by him is contained in the pages of a sketch book in possession of the Queen Victoria Museum and Art Gallery, Launceston.[1] The book probably dates from c. 1835. Three of the subjects are infants. The death of a child was a common occurrence in the nineteenth century; twelve percent of all children born in Van Diemen's Land in the 1850s failed to reach their first birthday.[2] It is perhaps ironic, therefore, that the offence for which Bock was lagged to this remote British penal colony involved a child that lived – rather than one that had died.

When he was in his early thirties Thomas Bock became infatuated with seventeen-year old Ann Yates. Despite being married with four children he persuaded her to leave her father's house for lodgings that he had procured for her. It was there, according to *Berrow's Worcester Journal*, that "he effected her seduction … gratifying his wicked inclinations".[3] When he discovered she was pregnant he persuaded her to drink oil of savin, a bitter and acrid poison distilled from the shoots of the juniper bush.[4] When this proved to have no effect, he persuaded her to take an even stronger draught, although this also failed to terminate the pregnancy. Ann Yates gave birth to a healthy child in October 1822.[5]

In his desire to conceal his sexual indiscretions, Bock put Yates at considerable risk. Savin is not a particularly effective abortifacient, although it is a dangerous drug the consumption of which produces vomiting and purging. It can be particularly damaging to the kidneys and accounts of the unpleasant demise of those who consumed it appeared in several nineteenth century medical journals.[6] In a much publicised case Charles Angus was tried for the wilful murder of Margaret Burns in 1808 after he had persuaded her to take savin.[7] If Yates had died, Bock would have been tried for murder. As it was, he was arraigned before the Warwick Assizes in Lent 1823 charged with "administering a drug to produce abortion".

He tried to wriggle free, instructing his defence counsel to defame the "poor creature he had thus cruelly used by insinuating that she was a common street-walker".[8] The judge was not impressed. He was particularly incensed that Bock was a father. Harriet, his eldest child had just turned seven while his youngest child, Thomas, had only just been born.[9] Far from being estranged from his family when he took up with Ann Yates, the recent birth of his youngest son in fact betrayed that he had switched between her bed and his wife's. The judge made it clear that if Ann Yates had died, he would have had no hesitation in passing a sentence of death with a strong recommendation that mercy should not be extended.[10] This was no idle threat; thirty percent of those found guilty at the 1823 Warwick Lent Assizes were condemned to death.[11] As it was, Bock was merely sentenced to a social death – exile for fourteen years to a far corner of the earth that would almost certainly guarantee he would never see wife, Charity, or his children again.

It is impossible to know the extent to which Bock was affected by the enforced removal from family. He had, however, lent a helping hand to the children of those less fortunate than him on a past occasion. When Luke Clennell, a pupil of Thomas Bewick, fell ill with severe depression in 1819, Bock was one of a handful of fellow artists who contributed funds to pay for an engraving of one of Clennell's works. The aim was to generate a source of funds to provide for the artist's three children.[12] Bock later was to give his services for free in order to help a friend repay a debt in Van Diemen's Land, and on other occasions is reported to have shown kindness,[13] but it is unclear whether the family he left behind, impoverished by his scandalous indiscretions, was provided for with a similar generosity. Later circumstances suggest not.

Bock sailed for Van Diemen's Land on the transport *Asia* in August 1823 arriving in Hobart Town on 19 January 1824. Convict artists often found themselves in demand in the penal colony. In Bock's case he was probably assigned to Dr Edward Bromley, a former naval surgeon who was a magistrate, treasurer of the Police Fund and director of the Bank of Van Diemen's Land.[14]

The penal colony operated as a form of open gaol. It could almost be described as a colonial work for the community scheme – except that the profits of convict labour often ended up in private hands. While some convicts were retained for government use, most were lent out to private settlers. There they worked without wages but were fed, clothed and accommodated by their citizen gaolers. Although masters of convict labour were not permitted to punish their charges directly, they could take them before a magistrates' bench to be tried for breach of the many regulations that governed convict service. Those found guilty could be flogged, sentenced to the cells or to hard labour in a road party or a chain gang. Short of death, the worst punishment was to be exiled to a penal station, the most remote of which was Macquarie Harbour located on Van Diemen's Land's isolated and dangerous west coast.[15] In Bock's case his colonial conduct record is blank. In the eight years he served as a convict he was never charged with an offence. This does not mean, however, that his passage through the convict system was incident free.

Soon after arrival in Hobart, Bock was put to work engraving a plate for a four dollar note for the Bank of Van Diemen's Land, a task which the assigned engraver completed in December 1824. The newspaper article that circulated the news of his feat referred to him as "Mr Bock", an unusual epithet for a recently arrived convict.[16] Mr Bock's services were in demand in other quarters too.

As a medical man Bromley was acquainted with the colonial surgeon James Scott. In fact, the two had arrived in Hobart Town from Sydney on the same vessel.[17] The connection resulted in the loaning of Bock's services for a rather more unusual task than engraving dollar plates. In late July 1824 the transported engraver found himself in the Hobart Hospital morgue, paper and pencil in hand. There stretched out before him was the recently executed corpse of the convict Alexander Pearce. Bock completed at least four sketches of Pearce, a man who had absconded twice from the remote fastness of Macquarie Harbour penal station surviving on both occasions through resort to cannibalism.[18]

Dissections were commonplace in Van Diemen's Land. The American convict, Robert Marsh, recalled that he once walked through the Hobart Hospital morgue door by accident and was appalled by what he saw: "In one place lay a leg, in another an arm, head, &c. &c.

Some bodies partly covered, others quite naked. Some pieces in boxes not covered, other boxes covered, ready to be carried away." It was not uncommon, he alleged, for coffins that contained the remains of up to three convicts to be interred in the cemetery.[19]

While there was no shortage of convict bodies to dissect, a cannibal was hard to pass up for those with an interest in phrenology – a belief that a person's character could be deduced as a result of an examination of their skull. Many Antipodean scientific minded gentlemen tried to make a name for themselves by documenting the local fauna and flora. A convict murderer who had preyed on his fellow absconders in order to keep himself alive was quite a specimen. Any account of a dissection required illustrations however. The services of William Buelow Gould, transported three years after Bock, were sought after by at least two collectors of botanical specimens for precisely this reason. All manner of things destined to be cut up by scalpels needed to also be rendered as images on a page in order for colonial discoveries to be adequately communicated to metropolitan learned societies.

Thus, it was that Bock completed the only surviving likenesses of Pearce, a man who had killed others so that he might survive. His offence in some respects differed little from the attempted crime for which Bock had been transported. The latter had not only sought to extinguish the life of his unborn child, but had put that of his teenage lover in jeopardy in a failed attempt to save his own skin. When Bock sketched Pearce's five foot three and a quarter inch frame laid out on the mortuary slab, did he contemplate how close he too had come to death by hanging?

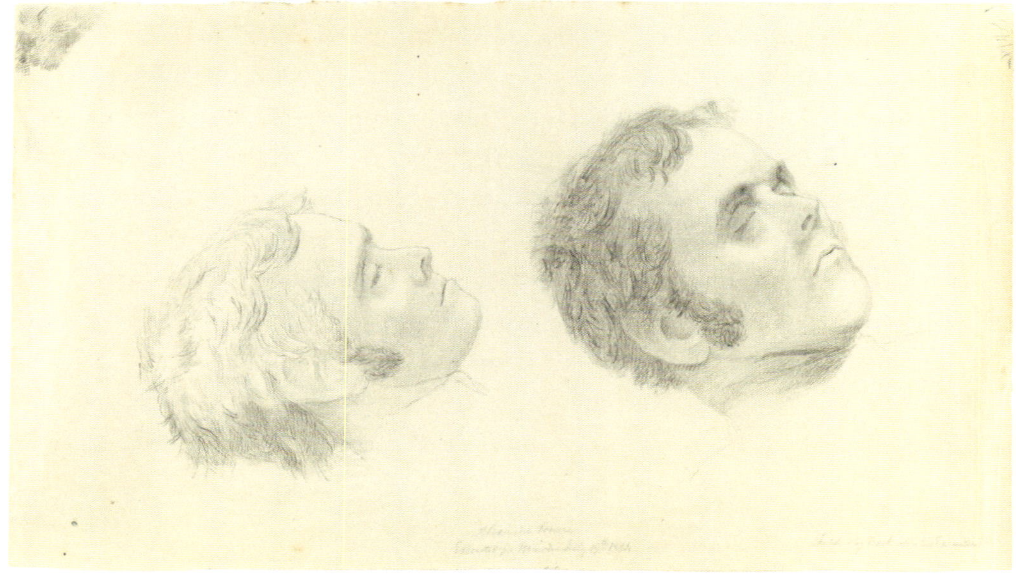

Alexander Pearce Executed for Murder July 19th 1824, 1824

After Bock had finished, Pearce's remains were cut up by at least two hands. It turns out, one of those who peeled back the flesh of the cannibal had quite a lot in common with Bock. Henry Crocket had been the surgeon at Macquarie Harbour but subsequently returned to Hobart Town to set himself up in private practice. Scott not only allowed his junior colleague to aid him in the task of dissecting the remains of a cannibal, but also he gave him permission to souvenir Pearce's skull.

In the following year Crocket married Emily Vardon in St David's, Hobart Town after she had accused him of being the father of her unborn child. Following the union he wrote to James Scott, to tender his resignation. "I feel it due to myself", he explained, "to assure you in the most solemn manner on the word of a man and the Honor of a Gentleman, that I am the victim of a deep laid and most infamous Plot; of which fact I can now from the mouth of Mrs Crocket most fully convince you."[20] As the marriage register reveals, however, Mrs Crocket was still very much a child. At fourteen years of age she was even younger than Ann Yates. That it transpired that she was not in fact pregnant counted for little in the scheme of things. "I cannot report that I have fallen a victim to conspiracy", Crocket wrote to Governor Arthur in a futile attempt to rescue the situation, "without wounding the character of her whom I have vowed to cherish, support and maintain."[21] In so doing, of course, he further sullied the reputation of the girl who had presumably been one of his patients.

His reputation in tatters, Crocket abandoned his young wife and slipped out of the colony taking Pearce's skull with him. He subsequently hawked the gruesome souvenir to William Cobb Hurry, a Calcutta-based agent who collected crania for the Philadelphia phrenologist Dr Samuel George Morton. The skull of the man Bock sketched now resides in the University of Pennsylvania Museum of Archaeology and Anthropology. The convict artist cannot have failed to have been struck by the similarities between Crocket's and his case, although as far as we know the colonial assistant surgeon had not attempted to induce the young Emily Vardon to consume a dangerous abortifacient.

Scandal also ruined the colonial reputation of Bock's master, Edward Bromley. In November 1824 it emerged that both the colonial revenue and the Police Fund, both of which he had charge, were several thousand pounds deficient. Although acquitted of embezzlement, it was apparent that Bromley's incompetence had enabled his convict clerk to make off with a large fortune. He was as G. T. W. B. Boyes the Colonial Auditor put it, thereafter "a ruined man".[22] With his master's fall from grace, Bock was shifted to another colonial household.

In the December 1825 convict muster he is listed as an assigned servant of the Deputy Colonial Surveyor G.W. Evans.[23] It is easy to see why a man whose work relied on cartography would be keen to acquire the skills of an engraver and artist; rather than pay an illustrator, Evans could draw on Bock's skills for free. The opportunity to commercially publish maps of the colony for sale presented a way of augmenting a colonial salary – and there were other ways of bolstering income.

Evans' patron, Lieutenant-Governor William Sorell was replaced by George Arthur – a devout evangelical Calvinist – in May 1824. Arthur later complained to the Secretary of State for the Colonies that he had not been in Van Diemen's Land for a fortnight before he started to receive complaints about "malpractices" in the survey department. When confronted with the allegations Evans retorted that the slurs were groundless, the slander having "originated entirely with disappointed persons". It soon became clear, however, that the surveyor had been in the habit of receiving "presents" from settlers and Arthur resolved to remove him from office, forcing him into early retirement.[24] Evans resigned in December 1825 on the grounds of ill-health and in November 1826 sailed for London,[25] and so Bock spent only a few months in his service.

While the December 1830 muster records that Bock was employed in government service, it is unclear if he was assigned in the intervening years.[26] It seems likely that his services were loaned informally, if not formally, to James Scott. In addition to the post-mortem drawings of Pearce, Bock sketched fourteen men who were placed on trial for capital offences between 22 July 1824 and 22 September 1830.

These sketches of bushrangers, the colonial term for an armed convict absconder, suggest an ongoing relationship with the Colonial Surgeon. Like the sketches of Pearce, three are post-mortem studies: John Godliman, executed 7 September 1825; James McCabe, executed 6 January 1826; and Charles Routley, executed 22 September 1830. If Bock had further access to the dissecting room in the Hobart Hospital, it was most certainly at the bequest of Scott. The Colonial Surgeon acted as a gatekeeper to the hospital morgue, barring entry to all but a chosen few.[27] Bock's drawings of Routley are particularly interesting since he also sketched the man's skull, revealing that he had access to the prisoner's remains post-dissection. Scott almost certainly commissioned this work.

Bock's bushranger studies appear to have been part of a grander enterprise. At least two are composites, worked up from courtroom sketches. While Bock drew James McCabe,

Matthew Brady and Patrick Bryant on the same page, their names printed neatly below each likeness, the three did not appear in court together. McCabe was tried on 5 November 1825 and Brady and Bryant on 25 April 1826. The same is also true of the sketch of Goodwin, Dunn, Hodgetts and Tilley. Dunn was executed on 18 November 1826 and the other three on 5 May 1826. The original working drawings from which these later composites have been fashioned also bear the names of each convict but written in italics rather than blocked out. There are several studies of the youthful Hodgetts. The last of these is much more heavily worked, almost as though it was being prepared for publication. Revealingly lithographs produced from three of Bock's studies of bushrangers survive. They include the profile of the dead Charles Routely positioned above his dissected crania.[28] It is unclear whether this was intended as an illustration for a treatise on phrenology or for wider commercial sale in an attempt perhaps to cash in on Routley's demise in a similar fashion to the manner in which Crocket had hawked Pearce's skull.

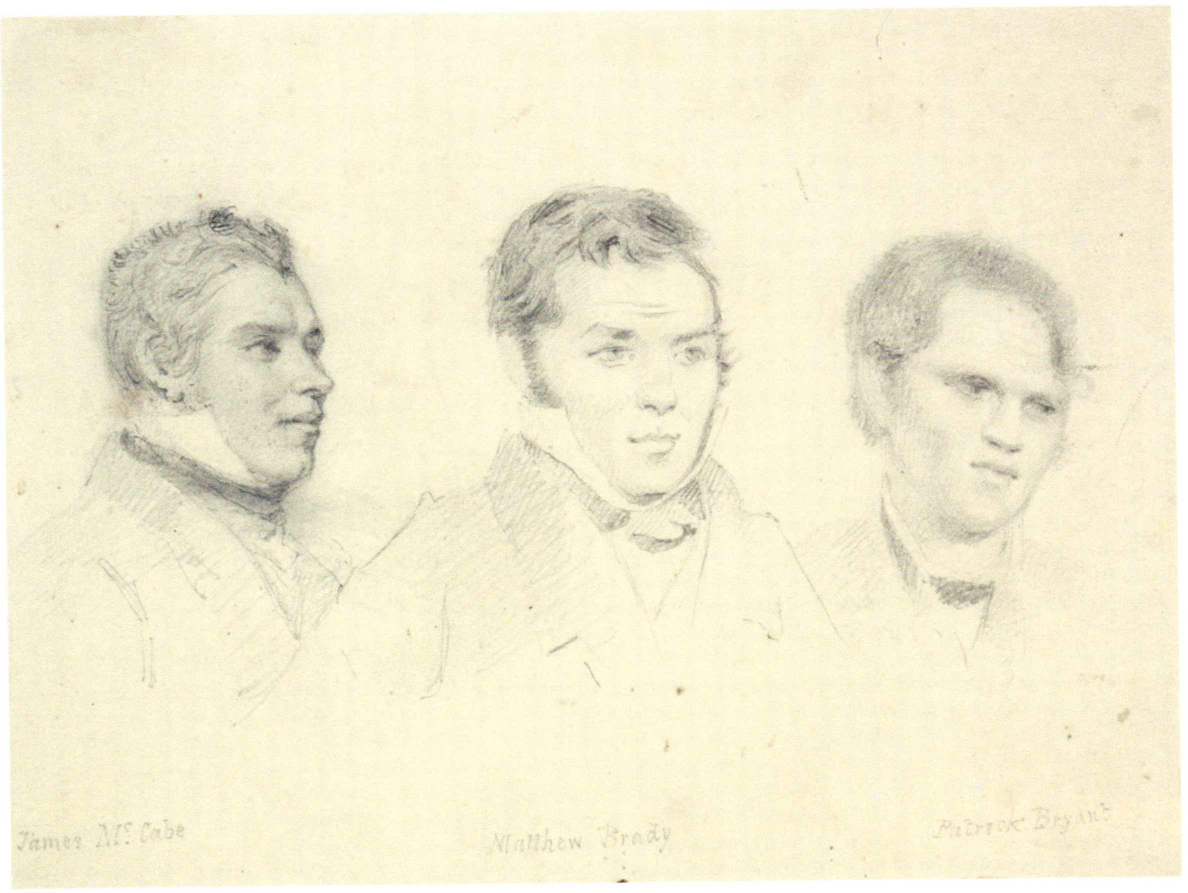

Sketches of Tasmanian Bushrangers, c. 1823–43

Many of the men Bock drew had acquired a degree of fame. Brady, who led the 1824–26 bushranging insurrection was supplied "with many little comforts" while in gaol awaiting trial and Dunne was followed to his grave by a cortege of about forty mourners, his dissected remains contained in a cedar coffin painted with a picture of Christ.[29] It was not unusual for clergymen to attempt to make money by publishing accounts of the last confessions of executed prisoners.[30] Images of celebrated bushrangers might be calculated also to find a ready market.

If anybody profited from this exercise it would have been Scott. All work completed by Bock during "government hours" would have been owned by his master. While Bock would have retained rights to any output completed in his own time (evenings, Saturday afternoons and Sunday) these were not the hours in which trials were held or bodies dissected. It is telling that none of these lithographs are signed by Bock. This is not particularly surprising. Plates made from illustrations completed by William Buelow Gould, appeared in *Curtis's Botanical Magazine* attributed to Scott, not Gould, although they were clearly produced by the convict servant rather than his master.[31]

Whatever their intended purpose, the bushranger sketches are remarkable for the manner in which each subject, dead or alive, is portrayed. Contrast Bock's rendering of the Irish convicts, Pearce, McKinney, McCabe and Bryant with Augustus Earle's depiction of "A Government Gaol Gang" outside Hyde Park Barracks.[32] Unlike Earle, Bock made no attempt to endow his subjects with simian features. Bock did not sensationalise those he sketched in the dock or laid out on the morgue slab, imbuing them with exaggerated brows designed to illustrate the finer points of phrenology.

All unfree labour systems are underpinned by ideology. In the case of colonial Australia, the justification for the exploitation of convicts was that each had been found wanting by a court of law. Arthur put the point bluntly in his defence of transportation: "Convicts, it is true, are not black, but white", he had argued "but they are *criminals*, and the master … may draw, from his knowledge of their crimes, a sanction, quite as satisfactory as that arising from difference of colour, for any severity he would practise against them."[33] The convicts Bock sketched were no ordinary members of the "felonry". Pearce had been likened in the colonial press to a vampire, while Brady and his fellow bushrangers were a "desperate body of … ruffians" who had committed "every species of enormity on the defenceless Settlers".[34] The striking feature of Bock's bushranger sketches, however, is the dignity he afforded his convict subjects. In this it is surely significant that the man who drew those who had been sentenced to death, had himself once been placed on trial for attempting to kill his own child. The felonry, as drawn by the felonry, stand in stark contrast to the descriptions of convicts penned by their gaolers and other moral entrepreneurs.

As the Queen Victoria Museum and Art Gallery sketch book reveals, after he received his conditional pardon in June 1832 Bock turned once more to drawing the dead. The dead, of course, made excellent subjects. They did not move or fidget, precisely obeying the artist's command to remain still. There are reasons why a man whose income relied on his ability to capture the likeness of those who commissioned works from him might like to keep his hand in by drawing the dead. It is thus possible that he continued to make studies of the deceased for reasons that were not dissimilar from those that drove the surgeons' desires to put their scalpels to work. Unlike the bushrangers he had drawn in earlier years, Bock did not name his dead subjects. Since even the infants are clothed, they are unlikely to have been drawn in a public morgue. These are not the bodies of the unclaimed, indigent poor. Several have been prepared for burial, a strap of cloth binding the jaw in order to preserve the dignity of the deceased. Although anonymous, the suspicion is that these are people close to Bock. How else would an artist have been permitted to observe the recently deceased if it was not without the permission of the grief struck living? One of those Bock drew might even have been his colonially born son.

The sketch book contains an inserted curator's note that reads, "the subject of this portrait is likely to be Edwin Morland Bock, son of Thomas and Marianne who died aged 13 (?) Information supplied by A.V. Bock 1968". Edwin Morland Bock was in fact aged 10 when he died of scarlet fever on 16 August 1853.[35] This son born to Bock's mistress, Mary Ann Cameron, bore the same first name as the child he had baptised in Birmingham in May 1821.[36] When Edwin Morland was christened did Bock know that the other Edwin was already dead?[37] In fact, by December 1845, all of the family he had been forcibly removed from as a result of the rash steps he had taken to try and cover up traces of his infidelity were in their graves.[38] It is likely that the demise of his wife and five British born children was hastened by the change in economic circumstances that followed Bock's enforced migration. It is possible that news of their demise was communicated across the world's oceans to the artist in colonial exile. He delayed marrying Mary Ann Cameron until July 1850.[39] This may well have been due to a reluctance to compound his earlier offence by committing bigamy. Whether convict or free the dead that Bock drew appear at peace. One suspects, however, that this was not always a peace that was shared by the artist who preserved their likeness on the page.

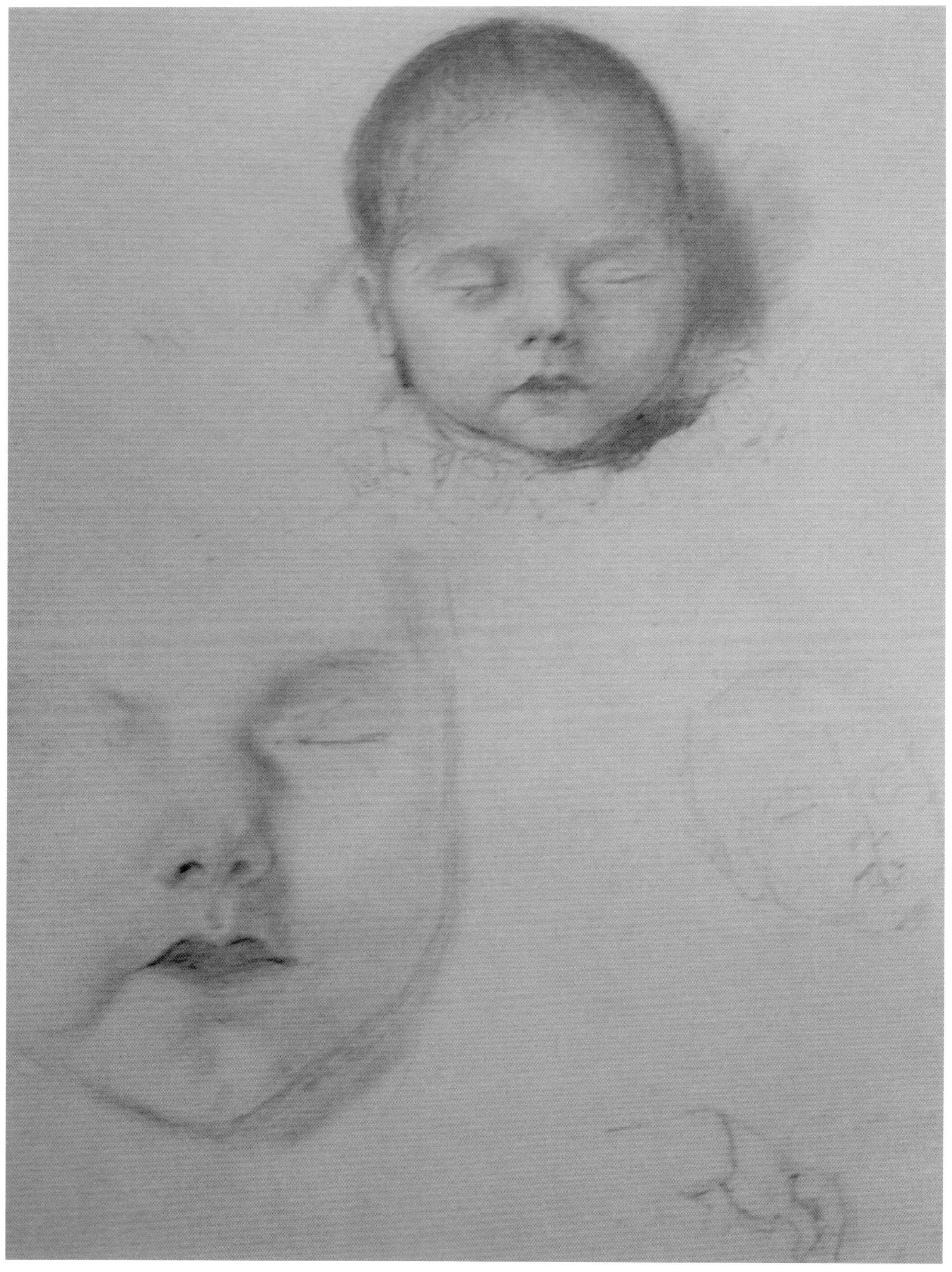

Page from **Sketchbook of post mortem studies**, c. 1835

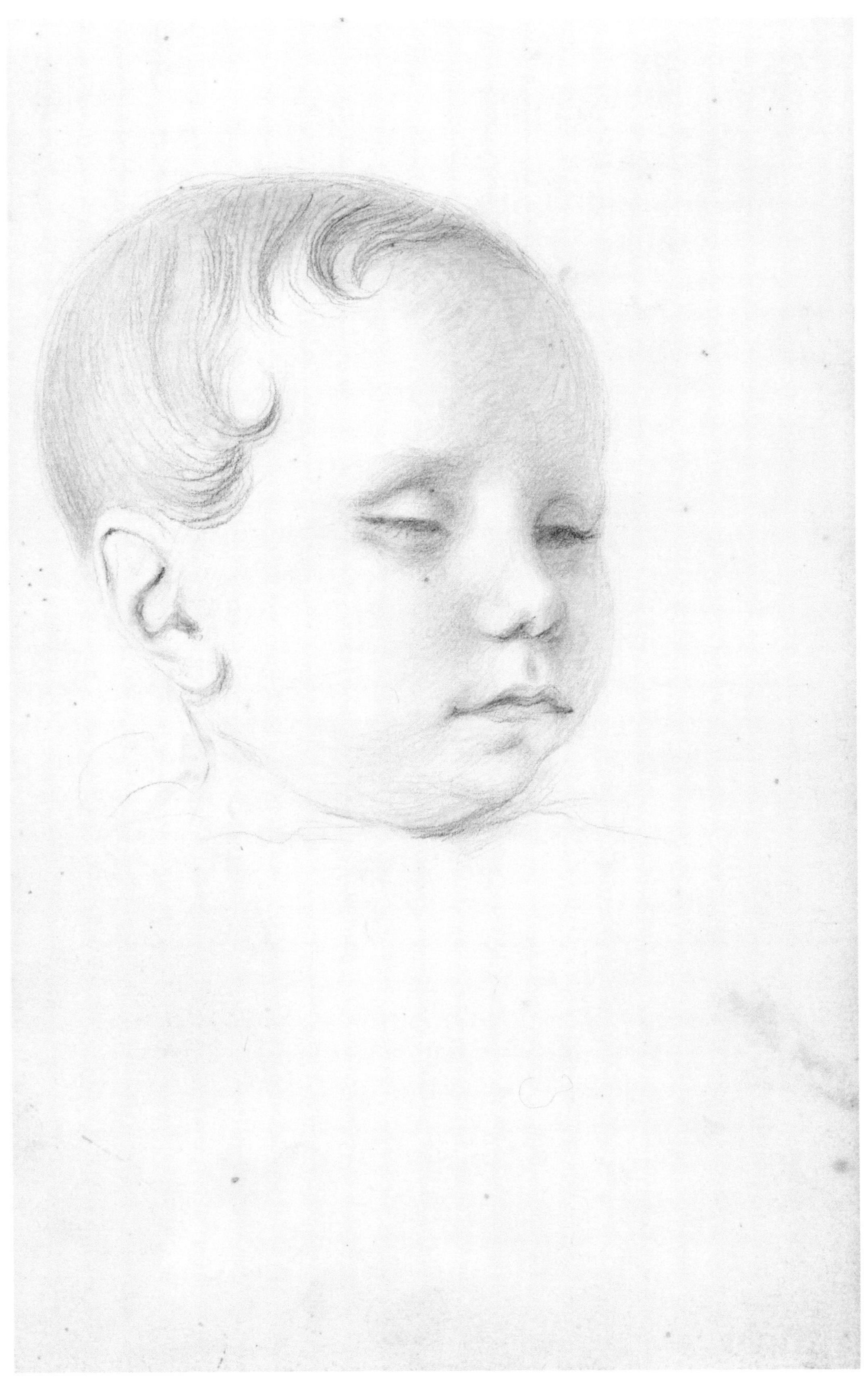

Page from **Sketchbook of post mortem studies**, c. 1835

1
Thomas Bock, Post-Mortem Sketch Book, Queen Victoria Museum and Art Gallery, QVM 1968.FD.3.

2
Rebecca Kippen, '"A pestilence stalks abroad": familial clustering of deaths during the Tasmanian scarlet fever, measles and influenza epidemics of 1852–1854', *Genus,* LXVII, 2, p.68.

3
Berrow's Worcester Journal, 17 April 1823.

4
Trewman's Exeter Flying Post or Plymouth and Cornish Advertiser, 24 April 1823.

5
Berrow's Worcester Journal, 17 April 1823.

6
The Western Journal of Medicine and Surgery, Prentis and Weissinger, Louisville 1846, p.440; *Associated Medical Journal*, 10 March 1854, p.294.

7
William Jones, *The Trial of Charles Angus, Esq. on an Indictment for the Wilful Murder of Margaret Burns,* Liverpool 1808.

8
Berrow's Worcester Journal, 17 April 1823.

9
Thomas Bock was born on 8 April 1823, Anglican Parish Records, Library of Birmingham DRO 25; Archive Roll M39, St Phillips, Birmingham, 1823, p.2.

10
Berrow's Worcester Journal, 17 April 1823.

11
England and Wales, Criminal Registers, The National Archive, UK (henceforth TNA), HO 27; Piece 26, pp.214–22.

12
'Proposals for Publishing by Subscription a Print Representing the Decisive Charge of the Life Guards at Waterloo by W. Bromley from a Picture by Luke Clennell', Thomas Underwood and George Underwood (eds), *The London Medical Repository, Monthly Journal and Review*, Volume 11, 1819, p.352.

13
Colonial Times, 28 September 1831.

14
Peter Chapman and Tim Jetson (eds), *Historical Records of Australia*, resumed series III, VII, Melbourne University Press, Melbourne 1997, p.612.

15
Hamish Maxwell-Stewart, 'Convict Labour Extraction and Transportation from Britain and Ireland 1615–1870, Christian de Vito and Alex Lichtenstein (eds), *Convict Labour: A Global Regime*, Studies in Global Social History, Leiden 2015, pp.182–93.

16
Hobart Town Gazette and Van Diemen's Land Advertiser, 10 December 1824.

17
Mary Nicholls (ed.), *The Diary of the Reverend Knopwood 1803–1838*, Tasmanian Historical Research Association, Hobart 1977, p.235.

18
Thomas Bock – Sketches of Tasmanian Bushrangers, ca. 1823–1843, State Library New South Wales, DL PX 5 and Thomas Bock, *Alexander Pearce Executed for Murder July 19th 1824*, State Library New South Wales, Dixson Gallery P2/21.

19
Robert Marsh, *Seven Years of My Life*, Buffalo 1849, http://iccs.arts.utas.edu.au/narratives/marsh6.html

20
Letter from Henry Crocket to James Scott Esq., 7 Oct. 1825, Tasmanian Archive and Heritage Office (henceforth TAHO), CSO1/95/2267.

21
Letter from Henry Crocket to Lieutenant Governor Arthur, 10 Oct. 1825, TAHO, CSO1/95/2267.

22
Peter Chapman (ed.), *The Diaries and Letters of G. T. W. B. Boyes*, Oxford University Press, Melbourne, 1985, p.214; Chapman and Jetson (eds), op. cit., III, VII: 718, note 94.

23
Entry for 713 Thomas Bock, TNA, 1825 Convict Muster, HO/10/46.

24
Chapman and Jetson (eds), op. cit., III, VII, p.88.

25
A. K. Weatherburn, 'Evans, George William (1780–1852), Douglas Pike (ed.) *Australian Dictionary of Biography*, Vol 1, Melbourne University Press, Melbourne 1966, pp.359–60.

26
Entry for 713 Thomas Bock, TNA,1830 Convict Muster, HO/10/47.

27
Helen MacDonald, *Human Remains: Dissection and Its* Histories, Yale University Press London, 2006), p.46.

28
Profile & scull [sic] of Charles Routley, Allport Library and Museum of Fine Arts, SD ILS:91942.

29
Eustace Fitzsymonds (ed.), *Brady: Van Diemen's Land 1824–1827*, Sullivan's Cove, Hobart 1979), pp.154 and 166.

30
Philip Rawlings, *Drunks, Whores and Idle* Apprentices, Routledge London 1992.

31
Eleanor Cave, '*Flora Tasmaniae*: Tasmanian Naturalists and Imperial Botany, 1829–1860', Ph.D thesis, University of Tasmamia, Hobart 2013, pp.122–23.

32
Augustus Earle, *A government jail gang, Sydney N.S. Wales*, National Gallery of Australia, NGA 95.344.

33
G. Arthur, *Defence of Transportation in Reply to the Remarks of the Archbishop of Dublin in his Second Letter to Early Grey by Colonel George Arthur*, George Cowie, London 1835, p.18. See also Hamish Maxwell-Stewart, '"Like Poor Galley Slaves": Slavery and Convict Transportation', Marie Suzette Fernandes Dias (ed.), *Legacies of Slavery: Comparative Perspectives* (Cambridge Scholars Publishing, Newcastle 2007), pp.48–61.

34
Hobart Town Gazette, 25 June 1824 and *Historical Records of Australia*, series III, vol. V: 28.

35
TAHO, Register of Deaths, RGD 35/1/4 No 342.

36
Edwin Bock, baptised 6 June 1821, St Philip's, Birmingham. Church of England Baptisms, 1813–1964, Library of Birmingham.

37
Edwin, son of Charity Bock, died aged 17 on 12 May 1838. Church of England Deaths and Burials, 1813–1964, Library of Birmingham.

38
Harriet Bock, Church of England Deaths and Burials, 1813–2003, Metropolitan Archives, St Luke's Chelsea, 11 September 1845; Emma Bock, Birmingham, Church of England Deaths and Burials, 1813–1964, Library of Birmingham, 3 January 1827; Adrian Bock, ditto, 30 August 1834; Charity Bock, ditto, 2 July 1844; Thomas Bock, England and Wales, Free BMD Index, 1837–1915, St George Hanover Square, Oct.–Dec. 1845, Vol. 1, p.3.

39
TAHO, Register of Marriages, RGD 37/1/9 no 363.

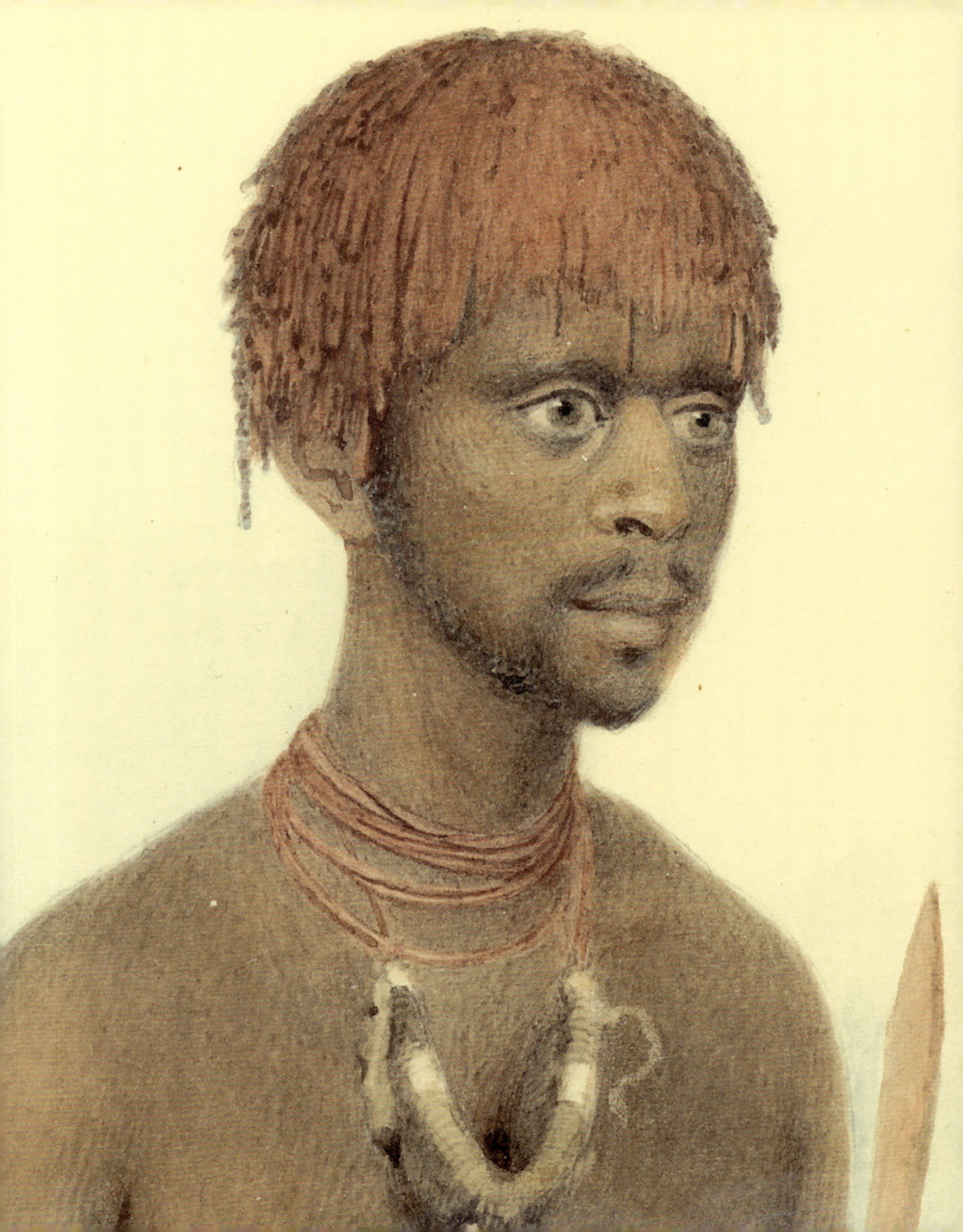

List of Works

Personal colour chart, undated
Watercolour
Presented by J Rogerson 1965
Courtesy Tasmanian Museum and Art Gallery
AG1401
p.4

Sketchbook, 1820s–40s
Presented by J Rogerson
Courtesy Tasmanian Museum and Art Gallery
AG1390

English landscape, early 1820s
Pencil on paper
Courtesy Allport Library and Museum of Fine Arts, TAHO

Sketches of Tasmanian Bushrangers, c. 1823–43
Album with drawings, lithograph, printed cards
Dixson Library, State Library of New South Wales
p.95

Alexander Pearce Executed for Murder July 19th 1824, 1824
Two pencil sketches on one sheet
Dixson Library, State Library of New South Wales
p.92

St David's Church, Hobart Town, 1824–35
Pencil on paper
Courtesy Allport Library and Museum of Fine Arts, TAHO
p.27

Sketch of a shed, 1824–35
Pencil
Presented by J Rogerson 1965
Curtesy Tasmanian Museum and Art Gallery
AG1400
p.26

Girl with arm extended, c. 1830s
Pencil on paper
Courtesy Allport Library and Museum of Fine Arts, TAHO
p.32

Half-length portrait of a young man, c. 1830s
Pencil on paper
Courtesy Allport Library and Museum of Fine Arts, TAHO
p.34

Half-length study, full face of a boy, c. 1830s
Pencil and crayon on paper
Courtesy Allport Library and Museum of Fine Arts, TAHO
p.33

Head of a man. Heavily scored in tracing, c. 1830s
Pencil on paper
Courtesy Allport Library and Museum of Fine Arts, TAHO
p.35

Woman with dark eyes, face finished with colour, c. 1830s
Pencil and watercolour on paper
Courtesy Allport Library and Museum of Fine Arts, TAHO
p.36

Sketch of Old Wharf, Hobart Town view from the commissariat store, 1830–55
Pencil on paper
Courtesy Allport Library and Museum of Fine Arts, TAHO
p.13

Commissariat Store or Hunter's Wharf, 1830–55
Pencil on card
Courtesy Allport Library and Museum of Fine Arts, TAHO
p.10

Murradanook, early 1830s
Pencil on paper
Courtesy Queen Victoria Museum and Art Gallery
QVM1975.61.10

Unknown man holding a spear, early 1830s
Pencil on paper
Courtesy Queen Victoria Museum and Art Gallery
QVM1968:FD:6H
p.61

Untitled, probably **Tukalunginta** (Togerlongerter), early 1830s
Pencil on paper
Courtesy Queen Victoria Museum and Art Gallery
QVM.1968.FD.6
p.17

Untitled, **Trukanini** (Truganini, Truggernana), 1831, later copy portraits labelled in error "Wortabowigee"
Drawing, watercolour
© The Trustees of the British Museum
p.74. Detail p.48

Untitled, **Wurati** (Woureddy), 1831
Drawing, watercolour
© The Trustees of the British Museum
p.75. Detail p.2

Untitled, **Namplut** (Numbloote, Jenny, Jinny), 1831–35
Drawing, watercolour
© The Trustees of the British Museum
p.85

Untitled, **Namplut** (Numbloote, aka Jenny), 1831–35
Drawing, graphite and watercolour
© The Trustees of the British Museum
p.79

Untitled, **Malapuwinarana** (Maulboyheenner, Timmy), 1831–35
Drawing, watercolour
© The Trustees of the British Museum
p.71. Detail p.101

Untitled, **Malapuwinarana** (Maulboyheenner, Timmy), 1831–35
Drawing, watercolour
© The Trustees of the British Museum
p.87

Untitled, **Manalakina** (Mannalargenna), 1831–35
Drawing, watercolour
© The Trustees of the British Museum
p.77

Untitled, **Manalakina** (Mannalargenna), 1831–35
Drawing, watercolour
© The Trustees of the British Museum
p.83

Untitled, **Prupilathina** (Probelatter, Lackerla, Jemmy, Jimmy), 1831–35
Drawing, watercolour
© The Trustees of the British Museum
p.81

Untitled, **Prupilathina** (Probelatter, Lackerla, Jemmy, Jimmy), 1831–35
Drawing, watercolour
© The Trustees of the British Museum
p.84

Untitled, **Tanaminawayt** (Tunnaminnerwate, Peevay, Jack), 1831–35
Drawing, watercolour
© The Trustees of the British Museum
p.80

Untitled, probably **Tanalipunya** (Tanleboneyer, Sall), 1831–35
Drawing, watercolour
© The Trustees of the British Museum
p.72

Untitled, **Trukanini** (Truganini, Truggernana), 1831–35
Drawing, watercolour
© The Trustees of the British Museum
p.86

Untitled, **Youth sitting**, 1831–35
Drawing, watercolour
© The Trustees of the British Museum
p.76

Cover of Van Diemen's Land Almanac for the year 1832, 1832
Engraving
Courtesy Queen Victoria Museum and Art Gallery
QVM1968.62.6
p.14

Untitled, probably **Multiyalakina** (Ehumarah, Umarrah), c. 1832
Watercolour drawing
© The Trustees of the British Museum
p.68

A Study of an aboriginal family, Henry Melville's Almanack, 1832–35
Grey wash on paper
Courtesy Allport Library and Museum of Fine Arts, TAHO

Untitled, **Laratung** (Larratong), 1832–35
Drawing, watercolour
© The Trustees of the British Museum
p.73

Untitled, **Wutapuwitja** (Wortabowigee, Fanny, Jock), 1832–35, later copy portraits labelled in error "Truggernana"
Drawing, graphite and watercolour
© The Trustees of the British Museum
p.78. Detail p.56

Untitled, probably **Muntipiliyata** (Montpelliater), c. 1832–35
Watercolour drawing
© The Trustees of the British Museum
p.70

Tukalunginta (Togerlongerter), c. 1832–35
Watercolour drawing
© The Trustees of the British Museum
p.69

Sketchbook of post mortem studies, c. 1835
Sketchbook – pencil on paper
Courtesy Queen Victoria Museum and Art Gallery
QVM.1968.FD.3
pp.28–29, 88, 98–99

Portrait of William Buelow Gould, c. 1839
Watercolour
Presented by H Westbrook 1941
Courtesy Tasmanian Museum and Art Gallery
AG711
p.39

Half-length portrait of female figure in house cap, c. 1840s
Pencil and crayon on paper
Courtesy Allport Library and Museum of Fine Arts, TAHO
p. 37

Interior view with woman sewing and child at right, c. 1840
Crayon with white highlights on tinted paper
Courtesy Allport Library and Museum of Fine Arts, TAHO
p.19

Reclining female nude, c. 1840s
Pencil heightened with white on paper
Courtesy Queen Victoria Museum and Art Gallery
QVM.1968.FD.20
p.46

Reclining female nude, c. 1840s
Pencil heightened with white on paper
Courtesy Queen Victoria Museum and Art Gallery
QVM.1968.FD.21
p.45

Reclining female nude, c. 1840s
Pencil heightened with white on paper
Courtesy Queen Victoria Museum and Art Gallery
QVM.1968.FD.28
p.47

Seated female nude, c. 1840s
Pencil heightened with white
Courtesy Queen Victoria Museum and Art Gallery
QVM.1968.FD.23
p.43

Seated female nude, back view, c. 1840s
Pencil on grey paper
Courtesy Queen Victoria Museum and Art Gallery
QVM1968.61.19
p.44

Study of a man's head, c. 1840s
Pencil on paper
Courtesy Allport Library and Museum of Fine Arts, TAHO
p.31

Woman and baby, c. 1840
Pencil on paper
Courtesy Allport Library and Museum of Fine Arts, TAHO
p.30

Woman and child at table, c. 1840
Pencil on paper
Courtesy Allport Library and Museum of Fine Arts, TAHO
p.20

Young woman with two infants, c. 1840s
Pencil and crayon on paper
Courtesy Allport Library and Museum of Fine Arts, TAHO

Mithina (Mathinna), 1842
Watercolour
Presented by J. H. Clarke 1951
Courtesy Tasmanian Museum and Art Gallery
AG290
p.53

Observatory, Domain, Sir John Franklin, Captain Crozier and Captain James Ross, RN, 1842
Watercolour
Presented by J Rogerson 1965
Courtesy Tasmanian Museum and Art Gallery
AG1391
pp.24–25. Detail p.6.

Woman in a bonnet: possibly Mrs Georgina Butler, 1845–55
Crayon, watercolour and opaque white on tinted paper
Courtesy Allport Library and Museum of Fine Arts, TAHO

James and Henry Barnard, c. 1850
Cased, hand-coloured daguerreotype
Presented by O Rodway 1943
Courtesy Tasmanian Museum and Art Gallery
Q610
p.40

Portrait of a gentleman, c.1850
Daguerreotype
Courtesy Queen Victoria Museum and Art Gallery
QVM.1996.P.0250

Two figures, possibly Downes and Charlotte Barnard, children of Tasmanian Government printer John Barnard, c. 1850
Cased, hand-coloured daguerreotype
Presented by O Rodway 1943
Courtesy Tasmanian Museum and Art Gallery
Q611
p.41

Thomas Bock

Ikon Gallery
6 December 2017–11 March 2018

Tasmanian Museum and Art Gallery
17 August 2018–11 November 2018

Curated by Jane Stewart and Jonathan Watkins
Assisted by Roma Piotrowska

Published by Ikon Gallery and the Tasmanian Museum and Art Gallery
Edited by Jane Stewart and Jonathan Watkins
Texts by Hamish Maxwell-Stewart, Gaye Sculthorpe and Jane Stewart
Designed by Herman Lelie and Stefania Bonelli
TMAG photography by Simon Cuthbert
Printed by EBS, Italy

Front cover: *Mithina* (Mathinna) (detail), 1842, p.53
Back cover: *Observatory, Domain, Sir John Franklin, Captain Crozier and Captain James Ross, RN* (detail), 1842, pp.24–25

The exhibition is organised in partnership between Ikon and the Tasmanian Museum and Art Gallery. It is supported by the Australian Government through the Australian Cultural Diplomacy Grants Program of the Department of Foreign Affairs and Trade, the John Feeney Charitable Trust, the Owen Family Trust, the Gordon Darling Foundation and a Jonathan Ruffer Curatorial Research Grant from Art Fund. Ikon is supported using public funding by Arts Council England and Birmingham City Council. The Tasmanian Museum and Art Gallery is supported using public funding by the Tasmanian Government.

Ikon Gallery
1 Oozells Square
Brindleyplace
Birmingham B1 2HS, UK
T: +44 (0) 0121 248 0708
ikon-gallery.org

Tasmanian Museum and Art Gallery
Dunn Place
Hobart TAS 7000
Tasmania, Australia
T: +61 (03) 6165 7000
tmag.tas.gov.au

ISBN: 978-1-911155-17-1

Distributed by Cornerhouse Publications
HOME, 2 Tony Wilson Place, Manchester, M15 4FN, UK
T: +44 (0) 161 212 3466 and +44 (0) 161 212 3468
email: publications@cornerhouse.org

Ikon Gallery Limited trading as Ikon
Registered charity no: 528892

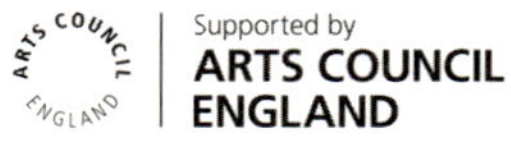

Supported by
ARTS COUNCIL
ENGLAND

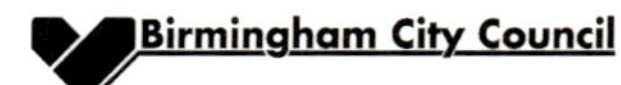

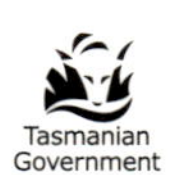

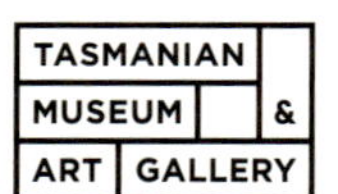

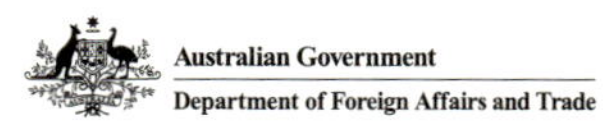

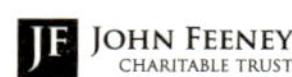

The Owen Family Trust

Art Fund_

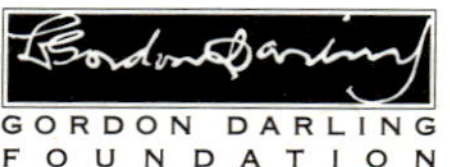